# Key Stage Three
# Shakespeare
# Romeo and Juliet

This book is for 11-14 year olds.

It's packed with all the really important stuff you need to know about *Romeo and Juliet* if you want to do well in your Key Stage Three SAT Shakespeare Question.

We've stuck loads of pictures and jokes in to make it more fun — so you'll actually use it.

Simple as that.

## What CGP is all about

Our sole aim here at CGP is to produce the highest quality books — carefully written, immaculately presented and dangerously close to being funny.

Then we work our socks off to get them out to you — at the cheapest possible prices.

# **Contents**

## SECTION 5 — WRITING AN ESSAY

## SECTION 6 — TYPES OF QUESTION

## SECTION 7 — THE SET SCENES

Published by Coordination Group Publications Ltd.

_Contributors:_
Taissa Csáky
Charley Darbishire
Samuel Datta-Paulin
Katherine Reed
Edward Robinson
Elisabeth Sanderson
Gerry Spatharis
Jennifer Underwood

_With thanks to Laurence Stamford and Paula Barnett for the proofreading._

ISBN: 978 1 84762 150 4

Groovy website: www.cgpbooks.co.uk

Jolly bits of clipart from CorelDRAW®
Printed by Elanders Hindson Ltd, Newcastle upon Tyne.

## Preparing Your Answer

Preparation is the key to doing well in your exam. So, before you start writing, plan what you're going to write. This will make everything a lot easier, even if it sounds like loads of extra work.

## You Have to Know the Set Scenes Really Well

1) The Shakespeare paper tests how well you know the play.
2) It's all about the set scenes. These are printed in full in Section 7 of this book.
3) You have to know these scenes like the back of your hand.

Learn your set scenes... or the puppy gets it.

You'll know which bits of the play you have to write about before the exam — which means you won't get any nasty surprises on the day. As long as you've learnt 'em, that is.

## Take Time to Plan Your Answers

Planning might seem like a waste of precious exam time. But if you just start writing without planning you'll end up spouting rubbish. Planning makes your answer loads better.

1) Read the question carefully. It will be based on your two set scenes (see section 7), so your answer will have to cover both of these scenes.

**e.g.** *Act 3 Scene 5 and Act 4 Scene 2*
*How does Juliet feel about marrying Paris in these scenes?*

For this question, you need to write first about Juliet's feelings in Act 3 Scene 5, then how her feelings have changed in Act 4 Scene 2.

2) Read through the scenes again. Look for anything the characters say that will help you answer the question. When you find something useful, underline it. E.g. For the question above you would look for anything that Juliet says about Paris.

3) Next, think about what the main points of your essay will be. Make a list.

**e.g.**
• *Juliet's feelings about Paris*
• *how these are affected by Juliet's feelings for Romeo*
• *how Juliet plans to avoid the wedding*

Do you see my point?

4) Include all your main points in the essay. Then you'll be on your way to a good mark.

## Preparation, that's what you need...

You'll feel a lot more relaxed once you've got a good plan to fall back on. Once that's sorted you can focus on each point one at a time. This makes the whole exam thing a lot less scary.

# Writing Well and Giving Examples

Examiners are a funny lot, but it's easy enough to <u>impress</u> them if you know what makes them tick. Here's a few <u>useful little tricks</u> that'll have them <u>gasping in admiration</u>.

## Use Examples to Show You Know Your Stuff

It's crucial that you use <u>examples</u>. They show <u>evidence</u> of the points you're making. As my old granny used to say, "An opinion without an example is like a boy-band without a rubbish dance routine." Or something.

<u>Quotes</u> are really useful examples. Examiners love 'em. Remember to:

1) Start and end quotes with <u>speech marks</u>.
2) Copy out the words <u>exactly</u> as they are in the play.
3) Keep it short — only quote the really <u>essential</u> parts that you need.
4) Explain <u>why the quote is a good example</u> — what does it tell you?

I couldn't unlock the key scenes.

## Sort Out Your Writing

1) Sound <u>enthusiastic</u> about the play. Use plenty of <u>adjectives</u> (describing words).

**e.g.** *The atmosphere in this scene is tragic and emotional — Shakespeare makes Romeo appear devastated through the combination of his powerful language and by setting the scene in a graveyard.*

2) Check your <u>spelling</u> and <u>punctuation</u>. Otherwise the examiner might not know what you mean.

3) Write in <u>paragraphs</u>. A page that's full of writing with no breaks is <u>tough to read</u>. Remember, <u>a new topic = a new paragraph</u>.

## Write About Versions of the Play You've Seen

If you've seen a <u>film</u> or <u>theatre</u> version of the play, you can write about that too — <u>as long as it relates to the question</u>.

This is another good way of sounding <u>interested</u> in the play. Just make sure you mention <u>which version</u> of the play you saw.

Keep in mind that each version can be very <u>different</u>. The <u>costumes</u>, <u>settings</u> and <u>personalities</u> of the characters can all vary.

**e.g.** *In the 2004 film version of the play, the director, Ivor Megaphone, shows the magic in this scene by using eerie shadows and the light of torches to illuminate the scene, and making Romeo's voice echo strangely.*

## I'll make an exam-ple of you...

Exams aren't really that complicated. They ask you a <u>question</u>, you <u>answer</u> it. If you're <u>prepared</u>, there'll be no nasty surprises. <u>Stick to the point</u>, and there's nowt to worry about.

## Stage Directions, Acts and Scenes

It's really important that you know what <u>stage directions</u>, <u>acts</u> and <u>scenes</u> are. Acts and scenes are like the <u>skeleton</u> of the play and stage directions tell you what's happening <u>onstage</u>.

## Stage Directions Tell You Who's Doing What

<u>Stage directions</u> tell the actors what to do, e.g. <u>when to come onstage</u> and <u>when to go off</u>. They sometimes say <u>who</u> they have to talk to as well. They're usually written in <u>italics</u> or put in <u>brackets</u>:

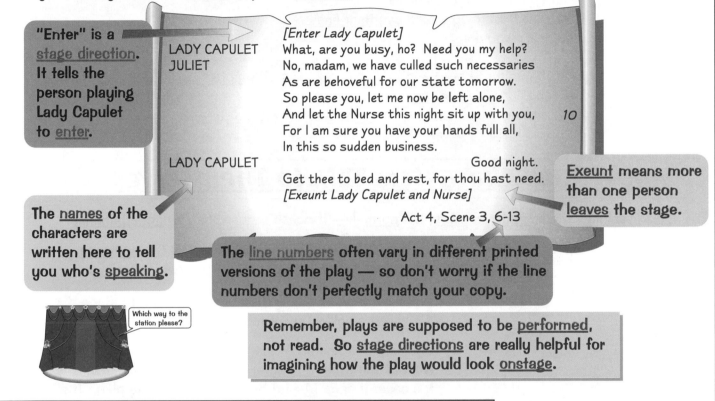

"Enter" is a <u>stage direction</u>. It tells the person playing Lady Capulet to <u>enter</u>.

LADY CAPULET
JULIET

*[Enter Lady Capulet]*
What, are you busy, ho? Need you my help?
No, madam, we have culled such necessaries
As are behoveful for our state tomorrow.
So please you, let me now be left alone,
And let the Nurse this night sit up with you,      *10*
For I am sure you have your hands full all,
In this so sudden business.

LADY CAPULET                                    Good night.
Get thee to bed and rest, for thou hast need.
*[Exeunt Lady Capulet and Nurse]*
                                   Act 4, Scene 3, 6-13

The <u>names</u> of the characters are written here to tell you who's <u>speaking</u>.

<u>Exeunt</u> means more than one person <u>leaves</u> the stage.

The <u>line numbers</u> often vary in different printed versions of the play — so don't worry if the line numbers don't perfectly match your copy.

Which way to the station please?

Remember, plays are supposed to be <u>performed</u>, not read. So <u>stage directions</u> are really helpful for imagining how the play would look <u>onstage</u>.

## Acts and Scenes Split Up the Play

1) The play is divided up into <u>five</u> big chunks called <u>acts</u>. Each act tells us <u>part</u> of the story. Put them all together and you get the <u>whole</u> story.

2) Acts are also divided up into even <u>smaller</u> chunks called <u>scenes</u>. Scenes <u>break up</u> the story. A <u>new scene</u> might be in a different <u>place</u>, at a different <u>time</u>, or with different <u>characters</u>.

   E.g. The first and second scenes of the play are set on <u>streets</u> in the city of <u>Verona</u>. The third scene is in the Capulets' mansion, then the fourth takes place a bit <u>later on</u>, outside the mansion.

Are you sure this is the right scene?

## Stop it, you're making a scene...

<u>Acts</u> and <u>scenes</u> are actually <u>really handy</u>, as they can help you <u>find</u> the speech or bit of action you're looking for. Remember — the play has <u>5 acts</u> and <u>loads of scenes</u>.

# Romeo and Juliet as a Play

Check out these <u>tips</u> and you'll really <u>get to grips</u> with the play.

## It's a Play, Not a Novel

It's meant to be <u>acted</u>, not just <u>read</u>. When you read the play, it's <u>hard to imagine</u> what it will look like <u>onstage</u>. Try to <u>see</u> the characters in your mind. Think about:

- what <u>kind of people</u> they are
- how you think they would <u>say their lines</u>
- how they would <u>act</u>

If you want some idea of how the play <u>might look</u> when it's <u>acted out</u>, you could watch it on <u>video</u> or <u>DVD</u>. Your school might have a copy of it — it's worth asking. Just remember: <u>each version will be different</u>.

## Sometimes Characters Talk to Themselves

1) In <u>real life</u>, this is <u>odd</u>. In <u>plays</u>, it's <u>normal</u> — it doesn't mean they've <u>gone bananas</u>.

2) The characters talk to themselves to let the <u>audience</u> know what they're <u>thinking</u> and how they're <u>feeling</u>.

3) When someone talks to themself on an <u>empty stage</u>, it's called a <u>soliloquy</u> (or monologue).

4) Sometimes a character may want to talk to the <u>audience</u>, without the <u>other characters</u> on stage hearing. If this is the case, it says <u>[Aside]</u> by their name in the play. It's as if the character is <u>whispering</u> in the audience's ear.

## Romeo and Juliet is a Tragedy

Shakespeare wrote <u>three main kinds of play</u>: tragedies, comedies and histories. Romeo and Juliet is a <u>tragedy</u>, but that <u>doesn't</u> mean the whole thing is meant to be tragic. Parts of it are witty and fairly <u>light-hearted</u>, but all Shakespeare's tragedies have a <u>sad ending</u>.

Most of the tragic bits are the scenes with <u>Romeo and Juliet</u>. They spend a lot of their time complaining about the fact that they <u>cannot be together</u> or <u>mourning</u> for the death of another character.

## Romeo, Romeo — How on earth doth I read this?

If you're not used to <u>reading plays</u>, it's bound to feel <u>odd</u> at first. The fact that some characters talk to themselves might seem bizarre, but it can help you to <u>work out</u> how they might be <u>feeling</u>.

# Odd Language

Some of this <u>old language</u> is hard to get your head round.  But once you get the hang of <u>reading it</u> things will become a lot <u>clearer</u>.  Just remember these <u>rules</u>:

## Don't Stop Reading at the End of a Line

1)  Follow the <u>punctuation</u> — read to the <u>end of the sentence</u>, not the end of the <u>line</u>.

**e.g.**
> One fairer than my love!  The all-seeing sun
> Ne'er saw her match since first the world begun.
>> Act 1, Scene 2, 92-93

There's <u>no full stop</u> here so carry on to the <u>next line</u>.

2)  This is only <u>one sentence</u> but it runs over <u>two lines</u>:

The all-seeing sun ne'er saw her match since first the world begun.

3)  Most lines start with a <u>capital letter</u> — but this doesn't always mean it's a <u>new sentence</u>.

4)  <u>Full stops</u>, <u>question marks</u> and <u>exclamation marks</u> show you where the sentence ends.

## Sometimes You Have to Switch the Words Around

1)  Shakespeare likes to <u>mess around</u> with the <u>order</u> of words.
It helps him fit the sentences into the <u>poetry</u> (see page 7).

2)  If a piece of writing looks like it's <u>back-to-front</u> — <u>don't panic</u>.
Here Juliet is talking about the risks Romeo is taking by coming to see her.

> If they do see thee, they will murder thee.
>> Act 2, Scene 2, 70

3)  <u>Play around</u> with the <u>word order</u> and it'll <u>make</u> a bit more <u>sense</u>.  What this <u>really</u> says is:

They will murder thee if they do see thee.

## Sense make doesn't Shakespeare...

I know Shakespeare's language looks really <u>different</u> from the English we write, but it's actually <u>pretty similar</u>.  Once you've got the <u>word order</u> sorted you're well on the way to <u>sussing it out</u>.

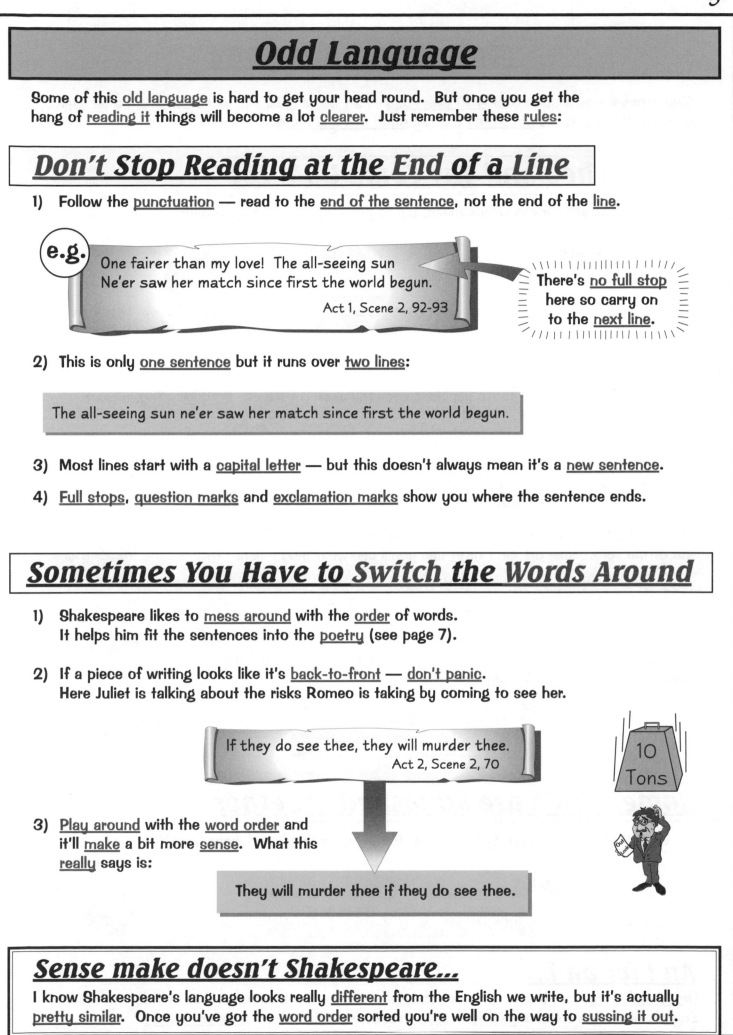

# More Odd Language

Shakespeare was around over <u>400 years ago</u> — so the language he uses can seem a bit <u>weird</u>. Some of the words are <u>old words</u> that we <u>don't use any more</u>.

## Thou, Thee and Thy Come Up a Lot

Once you know what these words mean, things get <u>a lot easier</u>. Happy days.

Thou = you

Thou wrong'st it more than tears with that report.
Act 4, Scene 1, 32

Thee = you

...the Prince will doom thee death
Act 3 Scene 1, 129

'Yea,' quoth he, 'dost thou fall upon thy face?
Act 1, Scene 3, 42

Thy = your

## Verbs Can Look Odd

Hast thou seen the size of this carrot?

Often, the difference is just a couple of <u>extra letters</u> on the end of the verb. Take off the <u>t</u> or <u>st</u> and you'll see what they mean.

**e.g.**

| | | |
|---|---|---|
| hath, hast = have | wilt = will | doth, dost = do |
| didst = did | thinkst = think | speakst = speak |

These verbs often go with <u>thou</u>, like this:

Dost thou not laugh?
Act 1, Scene 1, 174

## Some Words are Squashed Together

The word <u>it</u> often gets <u>stuck to the next</u> or the <u>previous word</u>, and <u>loses the "i"</u>.

'Tis an outrage!

**e.g.**

'twas = it was       'twere = it were
'tis = it is          is't = is it

## An i for an i...

<u>Dropping letters</u> from words isn't that strange when you think about it. We still do it in modern English, like when we change <u>it is</u> to <u>it's</u>. Shakespeare just drops <u>different letters</u>.

# Poetry

There's lots of <u>poetry</u> in Shakespeare's plays. If you understand the poetry, it'll <u>help you understand</u> some of the reasons behind the <u>strange language</u>.

## How to Spot Poetry

There's a lot of <u>poetry</u> in Romeo and Juliet — and <u>here's how to spot it</u>:

> Shakespeare's poetry has:
>
> 1) Capital letters at the start of each line
>
> 2) 10, 11 or 12 syllables in each line

A <u>syllable</u> is a unit of sound. The word <u>poetry</u> has 3 syllables – <u>po e try</u>.

## Poetry Doesn't Have to Rhyme

1) Some poetry <u>rhymes</u>, some <u>doesn't</u>.

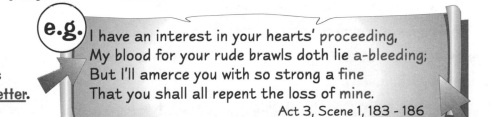

**e.g.**
I have an interest in your hearts' proceeding,
My blood for your rude brawls doth lie a-bleeding;
But I'll amerce you with so strong a fine
That you shall all repent the loss of mine.
Act 3, Scene 1, 183 - 186

Each line starts with a <u>capital letter</u>.

**e.g.**
I am the greatest, able to do least,
Yet most suspected, as the time and place
Doth make against me of this direful murder.
And here I stand, both to impeach and purge
Myself condemnèd and myself excused.
Act 5 Scene 3, 223-227

This bit of poetry is in <u>rhyming couplets</u> — the first line rhymes with the second, and the third rhymes with the fourth.

This <u>doesn't rhyme</u> — but it's <u>still poetry</u>.

2) The language sometimes sounds <u>strange</u> because Shakespeare tries to get <u>each line</u> to contain the <u>right amount of syllables</u>.

3) Most of Romeo and Juliet is written in poetry — although some of the <u>less posh</u> characters, like Nurse and Peter, talk in <u>prose</u> (speech that isn't poetry).

You did ask for three silly bulls?

## Look at the clock — Is that the Rhyme already?

Once you realise you're dealing with <u>poetry</u>, it becomes much easier to work out <u>what it means</u>. And the rules for <u>spotting it</u> are pretty simple — just remember that it doesn't have to rhyme.

# Revision Summary

Right, let's see how much you know about Bill Shakespeare and his odd little ways. If you haven't read any of Shakespeare's stuff before, it's easy to be flummoxed by the way he writes. But trust me, the more you read, the easier it gets. If you get stuck on any of these questions, look back through the section to find the answers. Then have another go, without looking back.

1) What's the point of stage directions?

2) What does "exeunt" mean?

3) How can you tell whose line in the play it is?

4) What's the play split up into?

   a) chapters and verses     b) nooks and crannies     c) acts and scenes

5) A play is meant to be:

   a) ignored     b) burnt     c) performed

6) Romeo and Juliet is a:

   a) tragedy     b) comedy     c) docu-soap

7) "A new line of poetry means it's a new sentence." True or false?

8) If a piece of writing doesn't make sense, what should you do?

   a) Change the word order     b) Phone a friend     c) Cry

9) When was Shakespeare around?

   a) 400 years ago     b) 200 years ago     c) 65 million years ago

10) What do these words mean?

   a) thou     b) hath     c) didst     d) 'twas

11) What does each line of poetry start with?

12) How many syllables are there in a line of Shakespeare's poetry?

13) Does all poetry rhyme?

14) What is "prose"?

# Who's Who in the Play

There are loads of characters in 'Romeo and Juliet'. Because the play is a tragedy some of them will die — but the real tragedy is that you have to know them all for the exam, so get cracking.

## Romeo — son of The Montagues

Romeo is the son of Lord and Lady Montague. He falls in love with Juliet (a Capulet). Their families are sworn enemies.

ROMEO

## Mercutio — Romeo's mate

MERCUTIO

Mercutio is Romeo's best friend and they are often hanging around together. He is fiercely loyal to Romeo.

## Benvolio — Romeo's cousin

BENVOLIO

Benvolio is Romeo's cousin and a friend of Mercutio. He doesn't like to fight and survives the play.

## Lord and Lady Montague

Romeo's mum and dad.

LORD M.  LADY M.

## Paris — Juliet's suitor

PARIS

Paris is a wealthy nobleman. He loves Juliet and wants to marry her. Lord Capulet is soon convinced that it's a good idea and so arranges for Paris and Juliet to marry.

## Juliet — daughter of the Capulets

Juliet is the daughter of Lord and Lady Capulet. She falls in love with Romeo, but her parents don't know about it and would never approve — so she marries Romeo in secret.

JULIET

## Tybalt — Juliet's Cousin

Tybalt (a Capulet) is a violent man and hates the Montagues — he is always looking for a fight, normally with Romeo.

TYBALT

## Lord and Lady Capulet

Juliet's mum and dad. They arrange for her to marry Paris.

LORD C.  LADY C.

## Nurse — Juliet's maid

NURSE

Nurse is Juliet's maid — she has looked after Juliet since she was born. She is very loyal to Juliet and would do anything for her. She also likes a drink.

## Friar Lawrence — a priest

Friar Lawrence is the local priest. He supports Romeo and Juliet's relationship.

FRIAR LAWRENCE

# Romeo

You need to do a bit <u>more</u> than remember Romeo's <u>name</u>. If you learn a few points about what he's <u>like</u>, you can mention them in character essays for <u>juicy marks</u>.

## Romeo's a Lover and a Killer

Romeo's a <u>romantic dreamer</u>... but he's got a more <u>dangerous</u> side too — he's <u>not afraid</u> to fight to the death.

Romeo's the <u>only son</u> of the Montagues, a <u>noble</u> Verona family. They're <u>constantly arguing</u> with the Capulets. It's <u>almost impossible</u> for Romeo to <u>avoid</u> getting involved in <u>fights</u>, because of the feud.

It's <u>more difficult</u> to be a lover. Romeo's <u>good</u> at it though. Everything he says to Juliet is charming, flattering <u>and</u> considerate.

## He Loses His Head a Lot — and Does Stupid Things

Romeo's <u>very passionate</u> — he's <u>full</u> of strong feelings. He <u>rushes</u> into whatever his <u>feelings</u> tell him to do.

1) The <u>first time</u> you see Romeo rushing into something is when he <u>falls in love</u> with Juliet. It happens <u>instantly</u> — and within 24 hours he's married to her. (Acts 1-2)

2) In Act 3, Tybalt kills Mercutio. Romeo's <u>furious</u> with <u>himself</u> that he let it happen, and furious with <u>Tybalt</u>. He <u>kills</u> Tybalt without stopping to think.

3) When Romeo hears Juliet's dead at the start of Act 5 he decides <u>at once</u> to go to Verona and poison himself.

4) If Romeo <u>slowed down</u> and <u>thought about</u> what he was doing he wouldn't get into so much <u>trouble</u>.

## He isn't Normally So Wet

You might think Romeo's a bit of a <u>drip</u>, but he isn't really <u>being himself</u> in a lot of the play.

In Act 2, Scene 4 Romeo's <u>joking around</u> with Mercutio and Benvolio. Mercutio is really <u>relieved</u> that Romeo's in a <u>good mood</u>:

> Why, is not this better now than groaning for love? Now art thou sociable, now art thou Romeo
> Act 2, Scene 4, 75-76

The Romeo his friends <u>know</u> and <u>love</u> is a lot more <u>fun</u> than the one we get to see.

## Romantic, passionate and fearless — *sigh*...

There are <u>loads</u> of things to say about Romeo. These are just a <u>few</u> of the main points to get you started. Remember, Romeo's not just a <u>slushy</u> character. He's a <u>fighter</u>, too.

# Juliet

You've got to know what Juliet's <u>really</u> like. Don't go thinking she's <u>drippy</u> and <u>feeble</u>.

## Juliet's a Capulet

The Capulets are another <u>wealthy</u> and <u>noble</u> Verona family — the Montagues' <u>enemies</u> in the feud.

I always get confused about who's from which <u>family</u>. This <u>rhyme</u>'s a great way to remember.

*Juli-ET*
*Capul-ET*

Juliet's only <u>thirteen</u> years old. She's definitely <u>not</u> a little girl — but she's young enough for some of the things that happen to be <u>mighty stressful</u>.

## She's One Tough Cookie

When Juliet meets Romeo she falls in love with him <u>instantly</u> and <u>completely</u>.
From that moment the <u>most important</u> thing for Juliet is to be with Romeo, but it <u>isn't easy</u>:

1) The biggest problem is that he's a <u>Montague</u>
   — a deadly enemy of the Capulets.

2) Juliet's parents have got plans for her to <u>marry Paris</u>. The <u>last thing</u> they'll want to know is that she's in love with a Montague.

3) Romeo can go wandering around Verona at <u>any time</u> of day or night. Juliet's not even allowed out of the house in the daytime without <u>permission</u>. She has to get the <u>Nurse</u> to organise her marriage <u>for her</u>.

4) In Act 3, Romeo kills <u>Tybalt</u> — Juliet's cousin and Lady Capulet's nephew. That makes it even more <u>impossible</u> for Juliet to tell her parents about Romeo.

## A Good Thing Too — She Has to Do Some Scary Things

Juliet can be <u>a bit soft</u> when she's with Romeo, but she does some <u>brave</u> things:

She risks cutting herself
off from her <u>family</u>.
Act 3, Scene 5

She takes a <u>sleeping potion</u>
knowing she'll wake up in a <u>tomb</u>.
Act 4, Scene 3

She gets <u>married</u> in secret.
Act 2, Scene 6

She kills herself, because she'd rather
be <u>dead</u> than alive <u>without</u> Romeo.
Act 5, Scene 3

<u>Some people</u> think Juliet's <u>immature</u> and gets <u>carried away</u> with love.
Maybe that's true, but you <u>can't</u> say the things she does are <u>easy</u>.

## Juliet's brave — she puts up with that Nurse...

I don't reckon Juliet's all that wet — there's more to her than meets the eye. Anyway, <u>you</u> can say <u>whatever you like</u> about her as long as you <u>back up</u> what you say with evidence from the play.

# Mercutio

I know it's a silly name, but Mercutio is probably the <u>coolest</u> character in the whole play.

## Mercutio is a Bit of a Star and Romeo's Best Mate

Mercutio is Romeo's <u>best friend</u>.

He's bursting with <u>energy</u> and always making jokes or <u>teasing</u> someone.

His speeches are full of <u>wordplay</u> and <u>crazy ideas</u>.

## He's Always Taking The Mickey

Mercutio calls Tybalt "Prince of Cats" and "rat-catcher" when he wants to wind him up. He's got the name from a story called <u>Reynard the Fox</u> — it used to be very popular. The <u>cat</u> character in the story was called <u>Tibalt</u>.

> Tybalt:    What wouldst thou have with me?
> Mercutio: Good King of Cats, nothing but
> one of your nine lives...
> Act 3, Scene 1, 72-74

Even when Mercutio knows he's <u>dying</u> he still makes <u>jokes</u>:

> Ask for me tomorrow, and you shall find me a grave man.
> Act 3, Scene 1, 92-93

*Mercutio's playing on the double meaning of the word "grave" ("<u>serious</u>" and also a place where you put <u>dead people</u>) — geddit!*

## Mercutio's the First Person to Die in the Play

When Mercutio's killed it leaves a <u>big gap</u> in the <u>play</u>. All that <u>energy</u> suddenly <u>disappears</u>. His death's really <u>sad</u> — it should <u>never</u> have happened.

1)  Tybalt didn't want to fight <u>Mercutio</u>. Mercutio gets involved because he thinks Romeo looks <u>cowardly</u> when he won't fight Tybalt:

> O calm, dishonourable, vile submission!
> Act 3, Scene 1, 69

2)  The fight is part of the <u>Montague-Capulet</u> feud. Mercutio isn't a member of <u>either</u> family. He blames the <u>feud</u> for his death:

> A plague a' both your houses!
> They have made worms' meat of me.
> Act 3, Scene 1, 101-102

3)  He also blames <u>Romeo</u>. He only gets hurt when Romeo <u>gets in the way</u> trying to stop the fight.

## Mercutio — doesn't that come before Venus...

The really important thing about Mercutio is he <u>fills up the stage</u> whenever he's on it with his nutty ideas and jokes. The jokes aren't all <u>side-splitters</u> but you can't say he doesn't try.

# Tybalt & Benvolio

You've got to get these characters <u>clear</u> in your head — <u>strange names</u> and all.

## Tybalt is a Troublemaker

Tybalt is Juliet's <u>cousin</u>, and Lady Capulet's <u>nephew</u>. He's always ready for a <u>fight</u>.
He fights Benvolio, Mercutio <u>and</u> Romeo. He fights to defend the <u>honour</u> of the family.

This is what Tybalt says when he sees
Romeo in disguise at the <u>Capulet party</u>:

> Now by the stock and honour of my kin,
> To strike him dead I hold it not a sin.
> Act 1, Scene 5, 57-58

## The Capulets Think Tybalt's Great...

Despite his <u>faults</u>, the Capulets
think Tybalt's <u>great</u>. Juliet, her
mum and the Nurse all say
they're <u>sorry</u> about him dying.

> Nurse: O Tybalt, Tybalt, the best friend I had!
> O courteous Tybalt, honest gentleman,
> That ever I should live to see thee dead!
> Act 3, Scene 2, 61-63

## ...But He Cheats When He Fights Mercutio

Tybalt shows his <u>sneaky side</u> when he kills Mercutio. He stabs him <u>under Romeo's arm</u>.
Mercutio could have thought the fight was <u>over</u>, or maybe he couldn't <u>see</u> properly:

> TYBALT under ROMEO's arm thrusts MERCUTIO in
> Act 3, Scene 1, stage direction, 85

## Benvolio's a Nice Bloke — He Doesn't Get Killed

Benvolio is Romeo's <u>cousin</u>, and a <u>good friend</u>.
He tries to do the <u>right thing</u> and stay <u>out of trouble</u>.

1) Benvolio always wants to <u>avoid fights</u>:

> I pray thee, good Mercutio, let's retire:
> The day is hot, the Capels are abroad,
> And if we meet we shall not scape a brawl...
> Act 3, Scene 1, 1-3

> Part, fools!
> Put up your swords — you know not what you do.
> Act 1, Scene 1, 56-57

2) Benvolio makes a <u>real effort</u> to cheer Romeo
up when he's feeling down about Rosaline.
He <u>persuades</u> him to go to the Capulets' party.

3) Benvolio tells Romeo to <u>run away</u>
after he's killed Tybalt, and stays to
tell the Prince what's <u>happened</u>.

## Tybalt = bad, Benvolio = good...

Tybalt and Benvolio are <u>very different</u>. Benvolio tries to be <u>sweet</u>, and Tybalt is definitely a <u>pain</u>.
Start off by remembering the <u>basic points</u> about them and the other stuff should <u>follow on</u>.

# The Parents

These are Romeo and Juliet's families. Make sure you don't get them <u>muddled up</u>.

## The Capulets Like Getting Things Their Own Way

Lord and Lady Capulet are Juliet's parents. They are very <u>ambitious</u>.

1) The Capulets are as <u>important</u> in Verona as the Montagues.
   Lord Capulet wants to make them even more <u>influential</u>.

2) Lord Capulet thinks he knows what's <u>best</u> for Juliet. After Tybalt's death in Act 3 he rushes to arrange the wedding to Paris to cheer Juliet up — in fact it's the <u>last thing</u> she wants.

3) When Juliet says she won't marry Paris, her father is so <u>angry</u> at her disobedience that he wants to hit her.

> My fingers itch.
> Act 3, Scene 5, 164

4) Lady Capulet is more concerned with Juliet's <u>social status</u> in marrying Paris than her <u>feelings</u>.

> So shall you share all that he doth possess,
> By having him, making yourself no less.
> Act 1, Scene 3, 94-95

5) Lady Capulet is <u>bloodthirsty</u>. She's quick to ask for Romeo's blood when he kills her <u>nephew</u> Tybalt. She dreams of having him <u>killed</u>.

> I'll send to one in Mantua...
> ...Shall give him such an unaccustomed dram
> That he shall soon keep Tybalt company
> Act 3, Scene 5, 88...90-91

## The Montagues are Nicer

Lord and Lady Montague are <u>Romeo's</u> parents.

1) Lord Montague is the <u>head</u> of the Montague family.
   The Montagues are one of the <u>richest</u> and <u>most powerful</u> families in Verona.

2) Lord Montague <u>worries</u> about Romeo when he's unhappy:

> Could we but learn from whence his sorrows grow.
> We would as willingly give cure as know.
> Act 1, Scene 1, 146-147

Lord Montague asks Benvolio to <u>find out</u> what's <u>wrong</u> with Romeo.

3) Lady Montague is a <u>gentle</u> and <u>emotional</u> person.
   She's very <u>concerned</u> about Romeo.

> O, where is Romeo? Saw you him today?
> Right glad I am he was not at this fray.
> Act 1, Scene 1, 108-109

4) When Romeo's banished to Mantua it makes Lady Montague so unhappy she <u>dies of grief</u>.

## They seem nice — but they're just as bad...

It's easy to think of the Montagues as goodies and the Capulets as baddies but it's <u>not</u> quite that simple. Don't forget the Montagues join in with the <u>feud</u> as happily as the Capulets do.

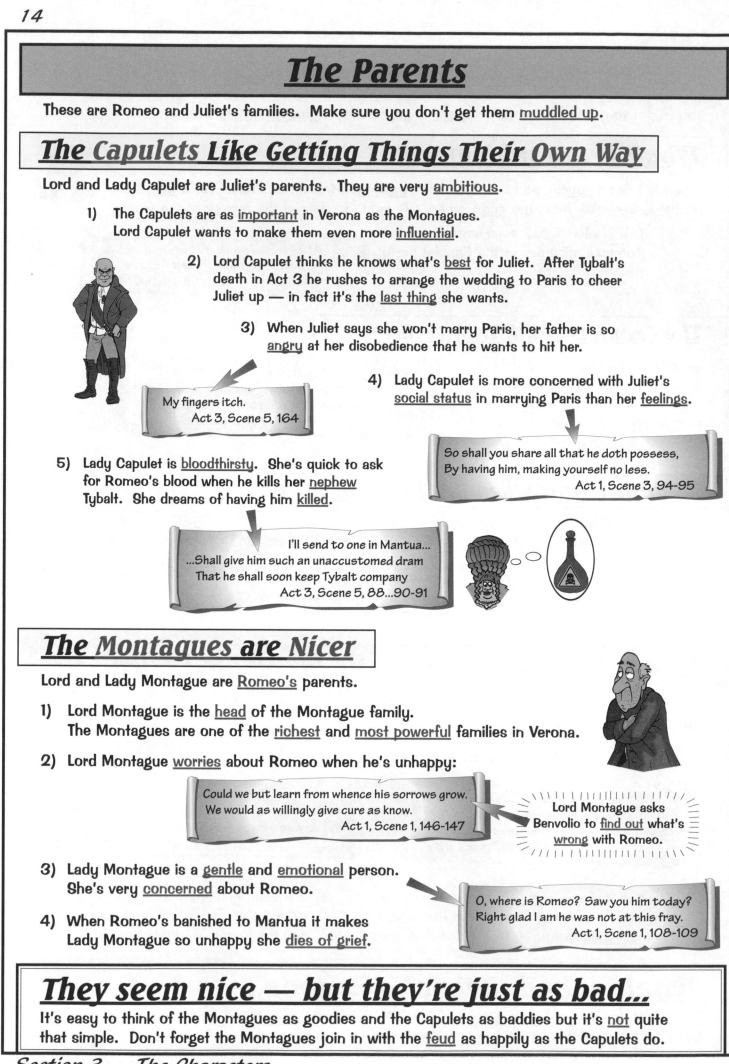

# The Nurse and Friar Lawrence

The Friar and the Nurse are the <u>only</u> people who know Romeo and Juliet's <u>secrets</u>.

## The Nurse is Not There Because Juliet is Sick

Let's get this clear <u>now</u> — the Nurse isn't a medical nurse. She's Juliet's nanny.
She's <u>looked after</u> Juliet since she was a baby. She even did the breastfeeding.
Lots of <u>rich families</u> employed nurses to <u>bring up</u> their children.

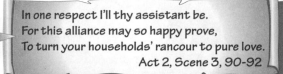

## The Nurse Really Loves Juliet

The Nurse is a <u>comedy character</u> — she's a bit of an <u>old windbag</u>.
She's very attached to Juliet, and does her best to help her.

1) The Nurse is more <u>affectionate</u> with Juliet than her mother ever is. She has <u>pet names</u> for her. In Act 1, Scene 3 she calls her a "lamb", a "ladybird", and a "pretty fool".

2) Juliet's a lot <u>closer</u> to the Nurse than she is to her mother because she's spent so much <u>time</u> with her.

3) When Juliet seems to be dead on the morning of the wedding to Paris, the Nurse is more <u>genuinely upset</u> than any of the other characters.

4) The Nurse has <u>no choice</u> about helping Juliet marry Romeo. Juliet's her <u>boss</u>.

> I am the drudge and toil in your delight...
> Act 2, Scene 5, 74

## The Friar Gives Advice to Romeo and Juliet

The Friar's <u>respected</u> for being an <u>educated</u> and <u>holy</u> man. He's <u>kind</u> and <u>thoughtful</u> but a bit <u>boring</u>.

1) A friar is a sort of <u>monk</u>, who does some of the things parish priests do — he can perform <u>weddings</u> and <u>funerals</u>, and people go to see him with their <u>problems</u>.

2) Romeo and Juliet go to the Friar for <u>help</u> and <u>advice</u> when they can't get it from their parents — when Romeo wants to <u>marry</u> Juliet, and when Juliet wants to <u>get out of</u> marrying Paris.

3) The Friar's <u>good</u> at giving advice. He persuades Romeo not to kill himself in Act 3, Scene 3, and talks Juliet out of killing herself in Act 4, Scene 1.

4) The Friar's <u>not</u> that keen to marry Romeo to Juliet — he knows all about Romeo's crush on Rosaline, so he <u>can't believe</u> Romeo's serious about Juliet.

5) He helps because he hopes the wedding will <u>end the feud</u>.

> In one respect I'll thy assistant be.
> For this alliance may so happy prove,
> To turn your households' rancour to pure love.
> Act 2, Scene 3, 90-92

## I'll let you into a little secret...

The Nurse and the Friar are good characters. They know <u>exactly</u> what's going on and help as much as they can — even though they <u>both</u> know things are likely to end <u>badly</u>.

# The Less Important People

Here's the <u>last lot</u> of characters to get to know, so get stuck in.

## Paris Wants to Marry Juliet

Paris is <u>conventional</u> and <u>polite</u> to everyone.
He keeps his emotions <u>hidden</u> — you never know how he feels <u>deep down</u>.

1) Paris is a <u>rich</u> and <u>influential</u> nobleman. He's related to the Prince who rules Verona.

2) That makes him a <u>useful ally</u> for Capulet in city politics. If Paris marries Juliet he'll be <u>family</u> and have to help Capulet — that's why Capulet's so <u>keen</u> on the wedding.

3) In Act 5, Scene 3 you see Paris at Juliet's tomb. He says he'll bring flowers <u>every night</u>. It's a <u>nice</u> thing to say, but he doesn't let his feelings <u>flood out</u> the way Romeo does.

4) When Paris is dying he asks Romeo to put him in the tomb <u>with</u> Juliet. That shows a <u>bit</u> more emotion. He probably <u>did</u> love Juliet, just in a <u>quieter</u>, <u>calmer</u> way than Romeo.

## Just Call Him Paris — Not Count or County

Paris's title is '<u>County</u>'. A County is the same thing as a <u>Count</u> — a <u>high-ranking nobleman</u>. Shakespeare <u>sometimes</u> calls Paris 'Count' and <u>sometimes</u> 'County'.

*Shakespeare uses 'Count' or 'County' depending on whether he wants a <u>one</u> or <u>two</u> syllable word to fit the rhythm of the line. If I were you I'd just call him <u>Paris</u> — it gets confusing otherwise.*

## The Prince is the Police-Chief, Judge and Jury

The Prince <u>rules</u> Verona. He always turns up to <u>sort things out</u> when there's been trouble or fighting. He decides <u>who</u> gets punished and <u>how</u>.

Even though he's really powerful he can't escape the <u>violence</u> of the feud. His <u>relatives</u> Paris and Mercutio both get <u>killed</u>:

> And I for winking at your discords too
> Have lost a brace of kinsmen.
> Act 5, Scene 3, 294-295

He speaks in really <u>formal</u> poetry — it makes him sound <u>posher</u> and more <u>powerful</u>.

## Don't Worry About the Other Characters

There are two other characters you should just learn the names of — <u>Balthasar</u> is Romeo's servant, and <u>Peter</u> is the Nurse's servant.

There are lots of other characters in the play — musicians, servants, and townspeople. You can think of them like <u>extras</u> in a film. They're just there for a bit of <u>padding</u> — so ignore them and <u>concentrate</u> on the stars.

### Paris — nice and polite but normal, boring and, ultimately, dead...

You <u>don't</u> need to know as much about these guys as you do about Romeo and Juliet — but you do need to know exactly <u>who</u> they are and <u>what</u> they do in the play. Get learning, sweetie.

# Revision Summary

*If you don't know who's who in the play it can get seriously confusing. You need to know the names of all the main characters — and how to spell them. What's more, you've got to know what they're like, and the main events they get involved in. Keep going through these questions, looking up ones you don't know, until you can answer them all without cheating. Answer them all, I said.*

1) Who are the deadly enemies of the Montagues?

2) Write down the full names of Romeo and Juliet.

3) What does Romeo do that shows he can be dangerous?

4) Complete the sentence: Romeo is...
   a) ...calm, level-headed and in control of his feelings.
   b) ...passionate, brave and a bit of a dreamer.
   c) ...a sports car.

5) Is Juliet a complete drip? Why? / Why not?

6) Who do Juliet's parents want her to marry?

7) List three brave things Juliet does in the play.

8) Would you say Mercutio is a) a bit of a laugh, or b) dull as ditchwater?

9) What are Mercutio's annoying nicknames for Tybalt?

10) Name Romeo's cousin and Juliet's cousin.

11) Write down two things Benvolio does to help Romeo.

12) Why does Lord Capulet want Juliet to marry Paris?

13) Does Lady Capulet think Juliet should marry Paris? What reasons does she give?

14) Does Lord Montague worry about his son? Give his reasons.

15) Why does Lady Montague die?

16) What is the Nurse's job?

17) Does the Nurse love Juliet?

18) What does Friar Lawrence hope will be the result of Romeo and Juliet's marriage?

19) When Paris is dying, what does he ask Romeo to do for him?

20) Who's the ruler of Verona?

## The Setting

The world Romeo and Juliet's set in is completely different from twenty first century Britain.
You don't hear Romeo complaining about rain, or the <u>rubbish on telly</u>, that's for sure...

### The Play's Set in Verona — an Italian City

1) Verona is a city in the North of Italy. In the play it's a <u>city state</u> —
a sort of small independent <u>country</u>. The <u>Prince</u> of Verona rules the
city like a King. He makes the <u>laws</u> and everyone should <u>obey</u> him.

2) Shakespeare probably <u>never</u> went to the real Verona — it just happens
to be where the story's set. It's based on an Italian legend in an old poem.

### There's a Feud Between Two Families in the City

There are two rich, powerful families in the play — the Montagues and the
Capulets. They're in the middle of a <u>feud</u> — a quarrel that's lasted for years.

The play <u>doesn't</u> tell us how the quarrel started. It's not <u>about</u> anything. It's a
<u>habit</u> the Montagues and Capulets have been brought up with. Now, they can't
stand each other. They only need a <u>tiny excuse</u> to start fighting.

In the Verona where <u>Romeo and Juliet</u> is set, it seems like <u>all</u> the men carry swords.
So if there's a <u>fight</u>, it isn't just a bit of a punch-up — it's a fight to the death.

### Everyone Cares About Honour

1) The characters in Romeo and Juliet have a strong <u>sense of honour</u>.

2) <u>Honour</u> is the <u>respect</u> you get from other people. If someone <u>insults</u> you they're
insulting your <u>family</u>, your <u>friends</u> and even your <u>boss</u>, so you <u>can't</u> ignore it.

3) <u>Right at the start</u> of the play, some servants of the Montagues and Capulets
meet in the street. They start insulting each other and it turns into a <u>fight</u>.

Draw, if you be men.
Act 1, Scene 1, 54          *Draw = draw your swords*

Any man who <u>doesn't</u> fight for his honour <u>isn't</u> a real man — he's a coward.

4) The feud is causing <u>deaths</u> and mayhem in Verona. In Act 1, Scene 1, the Prince of
Verona says he's had enough and the next person to start a fight will be <u>executed</u>.

5) But it's really hard for the Capulets and Montagues to give up the feud —
<u>honour is more important than saving lives</u>.

6) The <u>female characters</u> may not get involved in the fighting, but they <u>do</u> care about
honour and the feud.

### Hungry for a fight — must have more feud...

Tsk, tsk, that pesky <u>feud</u>, always causing <u>trouble</u>. It's all a bit like fights between the <u>mafia</u> or
different <u>gangs</u>. Not very nice in real life, but it makes for a <u>cracking story</u> in a film or a play.

# The Feud Affects Everything

When Romeo and Juliet fall in love it seems as though they can <u>escape</u> the feud, but that little delusion doesn't last long...

## Romeo and Juliet Know They're Taking a Risk...

1) When Romeo and Juliet fall in <u>love</u>, they're taking a big risk. It goes <u>against</u> the whole feud. Juliet warns Romeo <u>against</u> her <u>own family</u>:

> If they *do* see thee, they will murder thee.
> Act 2, Scene 2, 70

2) It's incredibly <u>dangerous</u> for them to be together — they have to get married <u>in secret</u>.

3) But there's hope that their love will somehow be <u>stronger</u> than the feud. Friar Lawrence agrees to marry Romeo and Juliet because he hopes it will <u>end</u> the fighting:

> For this alliance may so happy prove,
> To turn your households' rancour to pure love.
> Act 2, Scene 3, 91-92

## ...But the Feud is Inescapable

The feud creeps into every corner of the story. It all comes to a head in Act 3, Scene 1:

1) In Act 1, Scene 5, Romeo sneaks into the Capulets' party. Tybalt's furious and writes to Romeo, challenging him to a <u>duel</u>.

2) In Act 3, Scene 1, <u>Tybalt</u> meets Mercutio and Benvolio in the street. Tybalt tries to pick a fight with Mercutio. When Romeo comes along, Tybalt forgets Mercutio and wants to fight <u>Romeo</u>.

3) Romeo refuses. He's <u>just married</u> Juliet, so now he's related to Tybalt. Mercutio doesn't know about the wedding — he can't believe it:

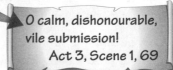

> O calm, dishonourable, vile submission!
> Act 3, Scene 1, 69

4) Mercutio decides to fight Tybalt <u>on Romeo's behalf</u>. Romeo steps in to stop the fight. He accidentally blocks Mercutio's view, and Tybalt <u>stabs</u> Mercutio under Romeo's arm.

5) Mercutio <u>dies</u>. Now Romeo's <u>too furious to care</u> that Tybalt is Juliet's cousin. He <u>has</u> to fight him to avenge Mercutio's death. Romeo wins the fight and <u>kills Tybalt</u>.

6) The Prince <u>banishes</u> Romeo from Verona — if Romeo's found in the city, he'll be executed.

<u>BEFORE</u> Act 3, Scene 1 it seems possible that Romeo and Juliet could see each other secretly, and admit to the marriage later on.

<u>AFTER</u> Act 3, Scene 1 it looks as if it's impossible for Romeo and Juliet to stay together. Mercutio and Tybalt are dead. Suddenly the feud and the play seem a lot more serious.

## Mercutio's death is such a waste — it's completely feud-ile...

The <u>feud</u> crops up everywhere — it's <u>central</u> to the plot. Even if your essay's not specifically about the feud, <u>at least give it a mention</u>. If you leave it out, you're kind of missing the <u>point</u>.

# Religion

Religion was a much bigger part of <u>daily life</u> when Shakespeare wrote 'Romeo and Juliet'. Lovely William made it a big part of the <u>play</u> too.

## The Church Had a Big Influence in the 16th Century

1)  In Shakespeare's time, <u>everybody</u> had to go to church on Sunday. Anyone who didn't go had to pay a fine.

2)  <u>No one</u> could get married <u>except</u> in church. Couples certainly couldn't <u>live together</u> unless they got married, and they weren't meant to <u>sleep together</u> either.

3)  Juliet <u>insists</u> on getting <u>married</u> to Romeo. She's not being <u>prissy</u> — for her it's the only option. If Shakespeare hadn't put in a marriage between Romeo and Juliet, the audience would have been <u>disgusted</u>.

## It's the Friar's Job to Look After Romeo and Juliet

The Friar is Romeo and Juliet's <u>confessor</u>. That means they go to him to talk about things they've done <u>wrong</u> and things they're <u>worried about</u>. It's his job to <u>forgive</u> people (in God's name) for the things they've done wrong, and give them <u>advice</u>.

1)  Romeo and Juliet can definitely trust the Friar. The Friar <u>isn't allowed</u> to tell anybody the things he hears in confession.

2)  They are going <u>against</u> their families and friends — the Friar is the only person they can talk to who <u>isn't involved</u> in the feud. They can't talk to their parents.

3)  The Friar's probably known Romeo and Juliet for years. He wants to help them on a <u>personal level</u> too.

4)  Marriage is <u>sacred</u> to the Church. Once Romeo and Juliet are married it's part of the Friar's job to protect their marriage.

But I've known Juliet since she was a teeny, weeny, lovely, cuddly little thing, wetting her...

SHUT UP, NURSIE!

Once Juliet's married to Romeo she <u>can't</u> marry Paris. If she did, she'd be breaking the <u>law</u> of the Church. That's another reason for Friar Lawrence to <u>help</u> Romeo and Juliet get away from Verona.

## Romeo Gets Sanctuary After Killing Tybalt

After Romeo has killed Tybalt, he goes straight to Friar Lawrence. That's because the Friar's the <u>only</u> person who's on his <u>and</u> Juliet's side.

There's another reason too, though. In Shakespeare's day, when someone <u>committed a crime</u>, they could go to a church and ask for <u>sanctuary</u>. So long as they stayed in the church they'd be safe from arrest — <u>if</u> they did what the church told them.

## Romeo & Juliet — a marriage made in... well, Verona...

When you're writing essays remember to <u>show off</u> a bit — show you understand the <u>religious reasons</u> for Romeo and Juliet getting married, and why Friar Lawrence tries to help them out.

# Family and Marriage

OK, things have changed since Shakespeare's time. You've got to remember that lots of these things weren't strange then, although they seem pretty bizarre now.

## Marriage Wasn't for Love — but for Money

1) In the 16th century, when the play was written, rich people like the Capulets or Montagues didn't get married for love. Their parents arranged a marriage with someone rich or powerful. It was a business deal — a way of getting more money and power into the family.

2) Men looking around for wives would prefer to marry a girl from a rich family. When her parents died the husband would get any money left to the daughter.

3) In 'Romeo and Juliet', Juliet is Lord Capulet's only heir. Her dad's meant to be loaded, so she would be quite a catch for Paris.

4) Normally the two people getting married didn't get much of a say. They were told they had to get married and who they were marrying.

## Capulet Wants to Choose Juliet's Husband

Juliet is only 13. In Act 1, Scene 2 Capulet says she's far too young to be getting married:

> Let two more summers wither in their pride,
> Ere we may think her ripe to be a bride.
> Act 1, Scene 2, 10-11

What does he think I am? A piece of fruit?

He also says that Juliet should have a say in whether she marries Paris.

This means — "If she agrees to marry you, I'll agree too."

> And she agreed, within her scope of choice
> Lies my consent and fair according voice.
> Act 1, Scene 2, 18-19

After Tybalt dies, Juliet is really upset because Romeo has been banished. Capulet thinks she's upset because of Tybalt, and decides a wedding's just the thing to cheer her up. When Juliet refuses, Capulet gets really angry, and tries to force her to marry Paris.

> I tell thee what: get thee to church a'Thursday,
> Or never after look me in the face.
> Act 3, Scene 5, 161-162

## Cowboy weddings — a-range-d marriages...

Arranged marriages were normal in Shakespeare's day. Lord Capulet's being pretty generous at first, when he wants Juliet to choose Paris for herself. More about Paris's character on p16.

# Family and Marriage

Juliet has it pretty tough in <u>Romeo and Juliet</u> — she's not expected to make any of the big decisions about her life. She's expected to just <u>knuckle down</u> and do what her parents say.

## Juliet is Supposed to Do What She's Told

1) Juliet's parents don't really <u>know</u> her very well — they don't have much clue about what she wants, and they <u>don't</u> really <u>care</u>. For <u>most</u> of her life, she's been brought up by the <u>Nurse</u>.

2) Juliet <u>isn't</u> even allowed out of the house <u>without</u> permission. She has to <u>send the Nurse</u> to take messages to Romeo — she <u>can't</u> go herself.

3) <u>Capulet</u> is in complete <u>control</u> of his family — he can tell Juliet to marry whoever <u>he wants</u>. She <u>isn't</u> supposed to marry without his permission.

## Juliet Breaks Two Rules When She Marries Romeo

1) Here's the obvious one — Romeo's a Montague and she's a Capulet. Both of them are going <u>against</u> the <u>feud</u> and <u>against</u> their <u>family's honour</u> by marrying an <u>enemy</u>.

2) Juliet's <u>disobeying</u> her parents — they want her to marry Paris, but she's marrying Romeo for <u>love</u>. They have to get married in <u>secret</u>.

Juliet doesn't get married because she <u>wants</u> to upset her family. She gets married because she wants to be with Romeo — and that <u>can't</u> happen unless they're married.

## Juliet's Forced to Lie to Her Parents

Juliet's parents would <u>disapprove</u> of everything she's done. She can't admit to <u>any of it</u> and that makes it even harder for her to explain why she <u>won't</u> marry Paris in Act 3, Scene 5.

1) When <u>Tybalt dies</u> and <u>Romeo is banished</u> her parents think she's upset about her cousin, Tybalt. She can't tell <u>them</u> she's upset because she can't see her <u>husband</u>.

2) Capulet decides he can cheer Juliet up by marrying her to Paris. She can't tell her dad that marrying Paris is <u>the last thing she needs</u>.

3) Juliet can't tell her parents she's got a <u>valid reason</u> for refusing to marry Paris, i.e. she's already married. Her parents think she's just <u>being difficult</u>.

When Juliet refuses to marry Paris, Capulet is so annoyed that he threatens to <u>throw</u> Juliet <u>out of the house</u>. He'd probably be even <u>more annoyed</u> if he knew what was really going on.

If Juliet wasn't <u>scared</u> of her parents she wouldn't have to go along with Friar Lawrence's risky scheme.

## The bwide's favouwite colour — wed, pewhaps...

All the <u>lies</u> Juliet tells are covering up the fact that she's married to a <u>Montague</u>. She knows what the rules are, and she'd rather not break them — but she has to because she's so in love. Aaah.

# Love

Here's another <u>cheery</u> page, about love, death and madness.

## Romeo and Juliet's Love Stands Out

1) Ideally love is <u>unconditional</u> and <u>lasts for ever</u> — or so they tell me at the movies.

2) Romeo and Juliet's love is <u>unconditional</u> — they'd rather die than lose each other.

3) In a weird way it's <u>everlasting</u> too, because they're both totally in love on the day they die — there's no time for <u>memories</u> to fade, or for them to think maybe the other one <u>isn't</u> perfect.

### ROMEO AND JULIET'S <u>LOVE</u> CONTRASTS WITH THE <u>HATE</u> OF THE FEUD

Their relationship contrasts with <u>other relationships</u> in the play:

Lord and Lady Capulet <u>genuinely believe</u> marrying Paris will be good for Juliet. They do love her in their own way, but they don't bother to find out what she <u>really thinks</u>.

Lord and Lady Montague are really <u>worried</u> about Romeo in Act 1, Scene 1, but they rely on <u>Benvolio</u> to sort it out. They love Romeo, but they <u>keep their distance</u>.

Paris and Lord Capulet treat love as a kind of deal — they don't go into the <u>emotions</u> at all.

The most <u>heartfelt</u> relationship apart from Romeo and Juliet's is the <u>friendship</u> between Romeo, Benvolio and Mercutio.

## Love Can be Destructive and Dangerous

Shakespeare doesn't <u>just</u> show love as <u>ideal</u>. He shows a <u>darker side</u> too.

1) Love is shown as a kind of <u>madness</u>: when Romeo's in love with Rosaline and being moody, Benvolio teases him, saying "Why, Romeo, art thou <u>mad</u>?".

2) In Act 2, Scene 6, Friar Lawrence is concerned that Romeo is <u>too deeply</u> in love, and warns him to keep control of his passions.

> These violent delights have violent ends...
> ...Therefore love moderately, long love doth so;
> Too swift arrives as tardy as too slow.
> Act 2, Scene 6, 9, 14-15

3) In a way even the <u>feud</u> is based on love. After the fight in Act 1, Scene 1, Romeo says:

The love and loyalty the Montagues and Capulets feel for their families <u>causes</u> violence.

> Here's much to do with hate, but more with love.
> Act 1, Scene 1, 167

## You Can View Romeo and Juliet's Deaths in Two Ways

Love made Romeo and Juliet <u>reckless</u> and <u>careless</u> — they put each others' lives in danger. If they hadn't treated love as the be-all and end-all they wouldn't have died.

**OR**

Romeo and Juliet were so in love they <u>had</u> to die. It was the <u>only way</u> for their love to be <u>perfect</u>. Their love was <u>so strong</u> that it brought the Capulets and Montagues together and <u>ended the feud</u>.

## So what's the problem? Love, Actually...

There isn't a <u>simple</u> answer to the question 'What did Shakespeare think about love?'. If you're writing an essay on ideas about love, mention as many as you can — there are plenty in 'Romeo and Juliet'. They don't all <u>tie up</u>, but that doesn't matter — this is a <u>play</u>, not a <u>physics formula</u>.

## What Happens in Act One

This section tells the <u>story</u> of the play. It shows you clearly what <u>every scene</u>'s about, so use it to get a complete overview of the <u>story</u>. And read the <u>text</u> — obviously.

## Prologue — The Whole Story in Fourteen Lines

**There's a feud going on in Verona**
The Montagues and Capulets are two of Verona's noble families. The families quarrelled years ago and are still feuding. The story's about two lovers, one from each family. They will both die, but their deaths finally bring an end to the quarrel. lines 1-14

The <u>quarrel</u> between the <u>Montagues and Capulets</u> affects <u>everything</u> that happens in the play and usually makes things <u>worse</u>.

<u>You know</u> right from the <u>start</u> that Romeo and Juliet are going to <u>die</u>.

## Scene One — The First Big Fight; Romeo's Being Drippy

The first big scene's got a <u>huge sword fight</u> — that's to make you sit up and pay attention.

You're so wet I could beat you with a spoon

**1 A fight starts**
Servants of the Capulets start a fight with servants of the Montagues by insulting them. lines 1-55

**2 Tybalt drags Benvolio in**
Benvolio tries to calm things down, but Tybalt forces him to fight. lines 56-64

**3 It turns into a street brawl**
The fight turns into a general brawl. Lords Capulet and Montague and their wives arrive. lines 65-72

**4 The Prince sorts it out**
The Prince stops the fighting and orders that the next person to cause trouble will be executed. lines 73-95

**5 What's up with Romeo?**
Romeo's parents are worried about him. Benvolio promises to find out what's wrong. lines 96-151

**6 He's in love and fed up**
Romeo tells Benvolio he is unhappy because he is in love with Rosaline, who doesn't love him. lines 152-230

Look out for Tybalt. Whenever he turns up in the play he causes <u>trouble</u>.

Calm it you lot...

Romeo's in love — with Rosaline. He <u>seems</u> dead serious about it.

Benvolio tells Romeo to <u>forget Rosaline</u> — there are plenty more fish in the sea.

The speech Romeo makes in lines 163-175 is full of <u>confusing opposites</u>:

Feather of lead, bright smoke, cold fire, sick health!
Still-waking sleep, that is not what it is!
(172-173)

...he's saying love is cruel <u>as well as</u> kind because Rosaline won't love him back.

# What Happens in Act One

It's no good <u>rushing</u> this section. In fact that's a <u>terrible</u> idea. It's all too easy to forget what went on <u>before</u> all the 'trouble' with Romeo. You get quite a different picture of old Capulet, for starters.

## Scene Two — Wedding Plans and Party Plans

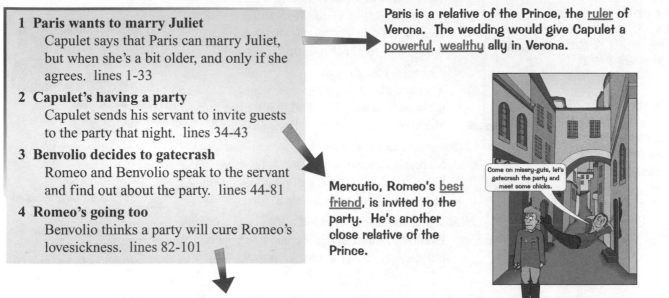

**1 Paris wants to marry Juliet**
Capulet says that Paris can marry Juliet, but when she's a bit older, and only if she agrees. lines 1-33

**2 Capulet's having a party**
Capulet sends his servant to invite guests to the party that night. lines 34-43

**3 Benvolio decides to gatecrash**
Romeo and Benvolio speak to the servant and find out about the party. lines 44-81

**4 Romeo's going too**
Benvolio thinks a party will cure Romeo's lovesickness. lines 82-101

Paris is a relative of the Prince, the <u>ruler</u> of Verona. The wedding would give Capulet a <u>powerful</u>, <u>wealthy</u> ally in Verona.

Mercutio, Romeo's <u>best friend</u>, is invited to the party. He's another close relative of the Prince.

Come on misery-guts, let's gatecrash the party and meet some chicks.

Rosaline's invited too. Benvolio thinks the <u>beautiful girls</u> at the party will take Romeo's mind off her.

## Scene Three — Juliet's Mother Tells Her About Paris

Juliet's mum and the Nurse think Paris is a real Mr Right — but Juliet's not so sure.

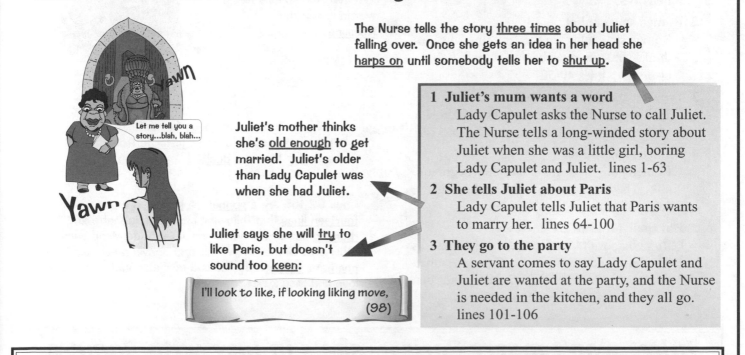

Let me tell you a story...blah, blah...

Yawn

Yawn

The Nurse tells the story <u>three times</u> about Juliet falling over. Once she gets an idea in her head she <u>harps on</u> until somebody tells her to <u>shut up</u>.

Juliet's mother thinks she's <u>old enough</u> to get married. Juliet's older than Lady Capulet was when she had Juliet.

Juliet says she will <u>try</u> to like Paris, but doesn't sound too <u>keen</u>:

I'll look to like, if looking liking move,
(98)

**1 Juliet's mum wants a word**
Lady Capulet asks the Nurse to call Juliet. The Nurse tells a long-winded story about Juliet when she was a little girl, boring Lady Capulet and Juliet. lines 1-63

**2 She tells Juliet about Paris**
Lady Capulet tells Juliet that Paris wants to marry her. lines 64-100

**3 They go to the party**
A servant comes to say Lady Capulet and Juliet are wanted at the party, and the Nurse is needed in the kitchen, and they all go. lines 101-106

# So why didn't he just stop after the prologue then...

You need to know all this <u>background stuff</u> — what Romeo was up to <u>before</u> he met Juliet, and how the feud's been going on for years and years — you're sure to need to refer to it somewhere.

## ACT 1 SCENES 4 & 5 — What Happens in Act One

Act 1 <u>ends with a bang</u> — Romeo meets Juliet, falls in love, then realises she's a Capulet...

### Scene Four — It's Party Time

Romeo and Benvolio <u>shouldn't</u> be going to a Capulet party — only Mercutio's been invited.

All the guests are <u>wearing masks</u> — it's easy for Romeo and his friends to <u>sneak in</u> to their enemy's party.

There are lots of times in the play where Romeo gets warnings of terrible events through <u>dreams</u> or <u>visions</u>. This is the first.

Guess who?

**1 Romeo's not in a party mood**
Mercutio, Benvolio and Romeo are about to go into Capulet's party. Romeo's friends are trying hard to cheer him up. lines 1-47

**2 He's had a bad dream**
They are about to go in when Romeo mentions a dream he's had that makes him afraid to go to the party. lines 48-52

**3 Mercutio takes the mickey**
Mercutio describes nightly visits of the fairy, Queen Mab, to all sorts of people, and the dreams she makes them have. lines 53-94

**4 But Romeo's still worried**
Even after the teasing, Romeo can't relax, but they go on to the party. lines 95-114

Did the fairy mention that perhaps the 'R' on your top might blow the disguise?

There's a point to what Mercutio's saying — he's <u>teasing</u> Romeo for paying so much attention to his dreams.

### Scene Five — Romeo <u>Annoys</u> <u>Tybalt</u> and <u>Charms</u> <u>Juliet</u>

**1 The party's getting going**
The servants clear up after dinner, and Capulet encourages his guests to dance. lines 1-39

**2 Romeo spots Juliet**
Romeo sees Juliet for the first time and thinks she's the most beautiful thing he's ever seen. lines 40-52

**3 Tybalt wants to fight him**
Tybalt spots Romeo, and wants to fight him. Lord Capulet tells him he can't. lines 53-91

**4 Romeo snogs Juliet**
Romeo goes up to Juliet and they begin to talk. They kiss, twice, and then the Nurse calls Juliet away. lines 92-110

**5 But their families are enemies**
Romeo doesn't know who Juliet is. He asks the Nurse and learns she's a Capulet. Juliet asks the Nurse who Romeo is and finds out he's a Montague. lines 111-143

It was only three scenes ago that Romeo said he was in love with <u>Rosaline</u>.

Phoarrrrrrr She's a babe!

ROMEO'S MASK

...but who's that guy with the big nose?

Uh-oh, it's Tybalt. He <u>obeys</u> Capulet here, but the next day he sends a <u>letter</u> to Romeo challenging him to a <u>duel</u>.

Lines 92-105 are a <u>sonnet</u>. A <u>sonnet</u> is a poem with <u>fourteen lines</u> that follows a strict poetic metre and <u>rhyming</u> pattern. Romeo and Juliet understand each other so well that even their first conversation is a <u>love poem</u>, or <u>sonnet</u>. By the end of the sonnet they are <u>in love</u> and they kiss.

### Juliet won't marry Paris — she's in love with Rome-o

Ooooh — it's all starting to get going... <u>That party</u> has a lot to answer for — and Romeo <u>shouldn't</u> have even <u>been there</u> in the first place. See — nothing good ever comes from gatecrashing. Except for meeting the love of your life. But she'll probably only die, so is it really worth it...

# What Happens in Act Two

You've met all the main characters and it's time for the story to really <u>take off</u>. This act's a bit more <u>lovey-dovey</u>. It's got that famous <u>balcony scene</u>. More fights to come in Act 3.

## Prologue — Time for a Recap

**The story so far...**
Romeo's forgotten Rosaline. Juliet's as much in love with Romeo as he is with her. They'll find it hard to meet. lines 1-14

## Scene One — Mercutio and Benvolio Call it a Night

Don't forget the <u>feud</u> — it's <u>dangerous</u> for Romeo to be in the Capulets' garden.

**1 Romeo wants to find Juliet**
Romeo breaks into the Capulets' garden, looking for Juliet. lines 1-2

**2 His friends leave him to it**
Mercutio and Benvolio look for Romeo, but can't find him and go home. lines 3-42

Not surprising really — it's almost <u>dawn</u>.

## Scene Two — It's That Slushy Balcony Scene... Yuck

This scene's <u>tense</u> and <u>rushed</u>. Romeo and Juliet could get caught <u>at any minute</u>.

**1 Romeo overhears Juliet**
Juliet comes out onto her balcony, not knowing Romeo's down below. lines 1-32

**2 She's talking to herself**
Juliet wishes Romeo wasn't a Montague, or that she wasn't a Capulet — because she loves him. lines 33-49

**3 Romeo speaks to her**
Juliet recognises Romeo and almost her first thought is that he's in danger. lines 49-84

**4 Juliet's a bit embarrassed**
Romeo's heard her say how much she loves him but she won't take it back because it's true. lines 85-106

**5 Romeo says he loves her**
Romeo tries to swear he loves her too, but Juliet feels everything is too rushed. The Nurse is calling her, and she goes inside. lines 107-141

**6 They talk about getting married**
Juliet comes back and suggests they get married. He promises to decide by the next day. They say goodnight and Juliet goes in. lines 142-189

Juliet's saying Romeo should stop being a Montague, or she should stop being a Capulet. That way they can <u>be together</u>:

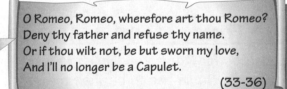

O Romeo, Romeo, wherefore art thou Romeo?
Deny thy father and refuse thy name.
Or if thou wilt not, be but sworn my love,
And I'll no longer be a Capulet.

(33-36)

Eh up pet, you look right nice!

You're not so bad yourself chuck.

## Rosaline — who's she?...

Learning the basics of each scene will make it easier to <u>understand the story</u>. You don't need to know the <u>whole thing</u>, but having a vague idea will help you understand how your set scenes fit in.

## ACT 2 SCENES 3 & 4 — *What Happens in Act Two*

The <u>cat's</u> out of the <u>bag</u>. Romeo <u>loves</u> Juliet and Juliet <u>loves</u> Romeo. We all know it's going to <u>end in tears</u>, so if I were you I'd enjoy the happy bits while they last. And <u>learn</u> the story.

## Scene Three — Romeo Books the Church

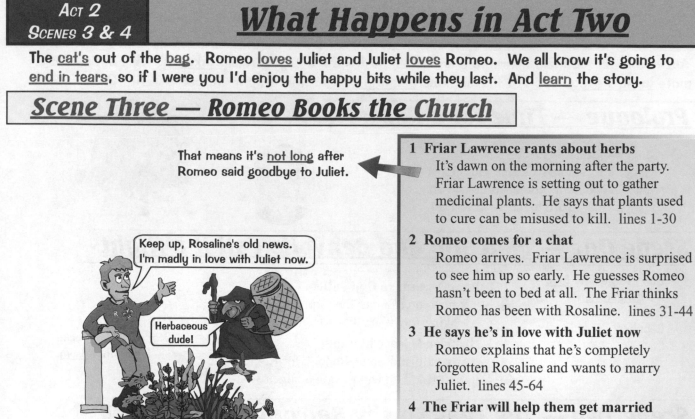

That means it's <u>not long</u> after Romeo said goodbye to Juliet.

Keep up, Rosaline's old news. I'm madly in love with Juliet now.

Herbaceous dude!

**1 Friar Lawrence rants about herbs**
It's dawn on the morning after the party. Friar Lawrence is setting out to gather medicinal plants. He says that plants used to cure can be misused to kill. lines 1-30

**2 Romeo comes for a chat**
Romeo arrives. Friar Lawrence is surprised to see him up so early. He guesses Romeo hasn't been to bed at all. The Friar thinks Romeo has been with Rosaline. lines 31-44

**3 He says he's in love with Juliet now**
Romeo explains that he's completely forgotten Rosaline and wants to marry Juliet. lines 45-64

**4 The Friar will help them get married**
Friar Lawrence is amazed how quickly Romeo's fallen in love again. Romeo says it's different now because Juliet loves him back. The Friar reluctantly agrees to the wedding. He hopes that the marriage will unite the two families and end the feud. lines 65-94

## Scene Four — The Nurse Takes a Bit of Stick

It's dangerous for Romeo and Juliet to meet in <u>public</u>.
That's why the Nurse has to be their <u>messenger</u>.

**1 Tybalt wants to fight Romeo**
Mercutio and Benvolio are talking about Tybalt's challenge to Romeo. lines 1-32

**2 Romeo's a lot happier this morning**
Romeo appears and Mercutio and Benvolio joke and fool around with him. lines 33-86

**3 Juliet's Nurse comes to see Romeo**
The Nurse arrives as Juliet's messenger, with her servant Peter. The boys think she's really funny and tease her. Benvolio and Mercutio leave. lines 87-123

**4 He tells her when the wedding is**
The Nurse is upset by the teasing. Romeo tells her the wedding will be that afternoon. lines 124-188

A "challenge" means a <u>dare</u> to fight a <u>duel</u>. Romeo will look like a <u>coward</u> if he doesn't fight Tybalt.

This is the first time Romeo's friends have seen him <u>cheerful</u> since the beginning of the play.

The Nurse is trying hard to be <u>posh</u> and taking herself a bit too <u>seriously</u>.

Wedding this afternoon.

Woof!

## No hurry — Romeo wasn't built in a day you know...

It's all starting to get <u>a bit serious</u> now — not just eyes meeting across a crowded room any more. They're about to cause <u>major mayhem</u> by getting married — hence all the <u>secrecy</u>...

# What Happens In Act Two

Two more scenes to go in this act, so make sure you get 'em <u>read and remembered</u>. The <u>clearer</u> you've got the play in your head, the <u>easier</u> it'll be to write about it.

## Scene Five — Good News for Juliet

**1 Juliet's in a bit of a tizz**
She's waiting impatiently for the Nurse. lines 1-17

**2 The Nurse brings the good news**
The Nurse arrives. She won't give Romeo's answer straight away and pretends she's exhausted from running the errand. Finally she tells Juliet that Romeo will marry her, and the wedding will be that afternoon. lines 18-77

The Nurse really <u>enjoys</u> being so important and being the <u>centre of attention</u>. That's why she <u>drags out</u> giving Juliet the message for so long.

There are no big preparations for the wedding. It's all got to be done in <u>secret</u>.

## Scene Six — Get Your Confetti Out

The cell is where the Friar <u>lives</u> — <u>not</u> a prison cell.

**1 The Friar gives some advice**
Romeo is waiting at the Friar's cell. Friar Lawrence says he hopes nothing bad will come of the wedding. Romeo says he doesn't care, because there is enough happiness in just a minute spent with Juliet. The Friar warns Romeo not to be so extreme — if he is a bit calmer his happiness will last longer. lines 1-15

**2 Here comes the bride**
Juliet arrives and all three set off for the church. lines 16-37

## Holy smoke — the deep fat Friar's gone up in flames...

Act 2 is the <u>happiest</u> part of the play, but there are still hints of <u>trouble</u> to come. In Scene 4 you find out Tybalt has challenged Romeo to a duel. There's no escaping that miserable feud. <u>Scribble down</u> the main events of Act Two from <u>here</u> and then from <u>memory</u>.

**ACT 3
SCENE 1**

# What Happens in Act Three

Well, I said there'd be <u>fighting</u> and here it is. Act Three is a real <u>mixture</u> of happy and sad bits. Mainly though it's where things start going <u>seriously wrong</u> for Juliet and Romeo.

## Scene One — Two Deadly Swordfights

There's lots of <u>action</u> in this scene — it's tricky to follow, so take it <u>chunk by chunk</u>.

**1 Benvolio's worried**
   Mercutio and Benvolio are out in the street. Benvolio thinks they should go home. Mercutio refuses and starts making jokes about Benvolio, saying he's a troublemaker. lines 1-31

**2 Tybalt comes looking for Romeo**
   Tybalt appears. He wants to fight Romeo but Mercutio starts teasing him. lines 32-52

**3 Romeo arrives but he won't fight**
   Tybalt tries to make Romeo fight but he won't. No one can understand why. Mercutio steps in. lines 53-71

**4 Mercutio will**
   Mercutio and Tybalt fight. Romeo tries to stop the fight by stepping between them. lines 72-84

**5 Tybalt stabs Mercutio**
   Tybalt gets a thrust under Romeo's arm and wounds Mercutio, then runs away. line 85

Benvolio <u>isn't really</u> the sort of person who starts fights, but Mercutio <u>enjoys pretending</u> he is.

Romeo won't fight because Tybalt is Juliet's <u>cousin</u>. He doesn't want to kill a <u>relative</u>.

Mercutio and Tybalt <u>don't know</u> about the wedding. <u>They</u> think Romeo's being a coward.

You alright back there Mercutio?.... Mercutio?....

Mercutio is really <u>angry</u> with Romeo for getting in the way.

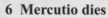

A plague a' both your houses! They have made worms' meat of me.
(101-102)

Mercutio curses <u>both</u> the Capulets and the Montagues. <u>Their feud</u> has killed him.

**6 Mercutio dies**
   Mercutio is badly wounded. His page goes for a doctor. Benvolio helps him to a nearby house. Moments later Benvolio returns — Mercutio is dead. lines 85-113

**7 Romeo kills Tybalt**
   Romeo is furious and upset. When Tybalt comes back Romeo is ready to fight. He kills Tybalt and runs off. lines 114-131

**8 Romeo's in big trouble now**
   The Prince, Lord and Lady Capulet and Montague arrive to find out what's been going on. Benvolio explains. The Prince banishes Romeo from Verona. lines 132-192

## Lovely motor, low mileage, one careful lady Verona...

There are so many important events in Scene 1, it's hard to know where to start. Mercutio dies, Tybalt dies, and Romeo gets banished to Mantua. It's no good just knowing <u>what</u> happens — you have to know the <u>order</u> it happens in. Scribble down a <u>quick list</u> for this scene and <u>learn it</u>.

# What Happens in Act Three

## Scene Two — Bad News for Juliet

In this scene Juliet gets so <u>upset</u> and <u>confused</u> she talks more to <u>herself</u> than she does to the Nurse.

**1 Juliet can't wait for the evening**
Juliet is happy and excited. She wants night to fall so Romeo can visit her. lines 1-31

<u>We know</u> Tybalt's dead and Romeo's banished, but Juliet doesn't. She's happy now but it <u>won't last</u>.

**2 The Nurse says Romeo's killed Tybalt**
The Nurse comes in very upset because someone's died. Juliet thinks Romeo's dead. At last the Nurse explains it's Tybalt. lines 32-72

Juliet is <u>worried</u> as soon as she sees the Nurse. By taking so long to explain, the Nurse gets her into <u>even more</u> of a state.

**3 Juliet can't believe it**
At first Juliet's shocked that Romeo could do something so evil. lines 73-85

**4 The Nurse criticises Romeo**
The Nurse agrees with Juliet that Romeo's done a terrible thing. Juliet gets angry with the Nurse for blaming Romeo. lines 85-96

**5 Juliet makes excuses for Romeo**
Tybalt would have killed Romeo so Romeo was right to kill him. lines 97-107

**6 She thinks she won't see him again**
Now Juliet thinks about the fact Romeo's banished and becomes hysterical. The Nurse goes to fetch Romeo. lines 108-143

Juliet's so unhappy at the end of the scene that she says she wants to <u>die</u>.

## Scene Three — Romeo's in a Real Mess

Romeo's pretty <u>upset</u>, and so he should be. From here on, his luck gets worse and worse.

It's no good I'm going to end it all.

Get over it you big Jessie!

Romeo's as <u>upset</u> as Juliet was in Scene 2.

The Friar's advice is all <u>common sense</u>. Romeo should behave like a man, and be pleased — he's alive, Juliet's alive, he was banished not executed, and Tybalt, his enemy, is dead.

**1 The Friar tells Romeo he's banished**
Romeo's at Friar Lawrence's cell. The Friar comes to tell him he's banished. Romeo says that's worse than death. lines 1-70

**2 Romeo says he'll kill himself**
When the Nurse arrives Romeo is ashamed he's killed Juliet's cousin. He threatens to kill himself. lines 71-109

**3 Friar Lawrence talks him out of it**
The Friar convinces Romeo that killing himself is pointless. He tells him to say goodbye to Juliet, then go to Mantua. lines 109-159

**4 Romeo goes to see Juliet**
Romeo leaves, happy and excited about seeing Juliet. lines 160-176

## Whoops...

Everything's getting <u>messy</u> — Juliet is upset cos Romeo has killed Tybalt. Romeo's <u>upset</u> cos he thinks he's ruined everything. Remember <u>what</u> they're upset about, and what they <u>decide</u> to do.

## ACT 3
## SCENES 4 & 5
# What Happens in Act Three

It strikes me this story is getting <u>mighty complicated</u>.
Skim back through this section to <u>check</u> the bits you're not clear about <u>before</u> you read on.

## Scene Four — The Capulets and Paris Set a Date

*Such a fine suitor for our darling daughter. I let him drink the last can of fizzy orange.*

*Oh so the last Tango's in Paris.*

Juliet's father has decided to get her <u>married off</u> as quickly as possible.

**Capulet says Paris can marry Juliet**
Lord and Lady Capulet are talking to Paris about his marriage to Juliet. Capulet promises that Juliet will marry him in three days' time. lines 1-35

## Scene Five — Seriously Bad News for Juliet

For all Romeo and Juliet know at this point everything's going to be <u>all right</u>.

**1 Romeo and Juliet say goodbye**
Early next day Romeo leaves Juliet for Mantua. They drag out saying goodbye, but eventually Romeo has to go. lines 1-59

**2 Juliet's mum comes to see her**
Lady Capulet comes in and finds Juliet crying. She thinks Juliet's crying for Tybalt. She also thinks Juliet's upset because Romeo wasn't executed. Juliet has to play along with this. lines 60-103

**3 She says Juliet's got to marry Paris**
To cheer Juliet up Lady Capulet tells her about the marriage to Paris. Juliet says she won't marry Paris — that she would rather marry Romeo. lines 104-125

**4 Juliet's dad says he'll force her**
Lord Capulet arrives and tells Juliet to pull herself together. He quickly loses patience. Both Juliet's parents are furious and leave. lines 126-195

**5 The Nurse tells Juliet to marry Paris**
Juliet asks for the Nurse's help, but she sides with Juliet's parents. Juliet's furious and decides to see the Friar. If she has no better option she'll kill herself. lines 196-242

*There's a voice, keeps on calling me, down the road, that's where I'll always be...*

Mantua
Verona

Juliet can't marry Paris — she's <u>already married</u>. If she gets married again she'll be <u>breaking</u> the city's laws and Church <u>law</u>.

Lord Capulet is <u>really harsh</u> in this scene. He tells Juliet he will throw her out if she doesn't marry Paris.

Lady Capulet isn't as cross — she just thinks Juliet is being <u>stupid</u> to refuse such a good marriage.

Juliet's having a terrible time and not even the <u>Nurse</u> will support her.

*Rooooooarrrrrrrrrrrrrrrrrr*

# Bigamy or suicide — not the best choice in the world...

Romeo's best friend's <u>dead</u>. Romeo and Juliet are married but <u>can't</u> be together for more than a night. Juliet's being made to <u>marry</u> someone she doesn't even know. Not a very cheerful act really. <u>Learn</u> all the <u>main events</u> — it's sad stuff, but it's all important.

# What Happens in Act Four

**ACT 4**
**SCENES 1, 2 & 3**

Act Four's <u>not</u> even slightly <u>happy</u>, but the story's <u>not hard</u> to follow — Juliet's parents are <u>frantic</u> to get her married to Paris and Juliet does <u>everything</u> she can to get out of it.

## Scene One — Friar Lawrence's Cunning Plan

**1 Paris is arranging his wedding**
Paris is talking to the Friar. lines 1-17

Paris says Capulet arranged the wedding to <u>cheer Juliet up</u>.

**2 Juliet arrives as Paris is leaving**
She's polite but distant. He tries to be friendly. lines 18-43

Friar Lawrence is in a <u>tricky position</u>. He can't let Juliet get married twice, and he can't let on about Romeo and Juliet.

**3 Juliet won't marry Paris**
Juliet tells the Friar she would rather kill herself than marry Paris. lines 44-67

Paris <u>thinks</u> Juliet wants to marry him.

**4 The Friar's got a plan**
Friar Lawrence sees she's deadly serious and makes a plan. Juliet will take a sleeping potion that makes her look dead. After she's buried, Romeo will come and rescue her. Juliet agrees to the plan. lines 68-126

After being <u>cold and polite</u> with Paris, Juliet gets very emotional and shows her <u>real feelings</u>.

> Do you know you're the spitting image of Yoda?

## Scene Two — Juliet Plays the Dutiful Daughter

This is one of the shortest scenes in the play — but that doesn't mean it's not <u>important</u>.

**1 Capulet's organising the wedding**
The Capulet household is preparing for the wedding. lines 1-13

The wedding's going ahead even though Juliet has <u>never agreed</u> to marry Paris.

**2 Juliet agrees to marry Paris**
Juliet comes back from the Friar's. She tells her parents she's sorry she was disobedient and that she'll marry Paris. lines 14-47

> Of course I'll marry Paris...
> ...not.

## Scene Three — A Spoonful of Sugar...

**1 Juliet has an early night**
Juliet's Nurse and mother want to help her get ready for the wedding, but Juliet says she needs to sleep and says goodnight. lines 1-13

She's got a <u>dagger</u> just in case.

It's like Romeo's dreams — a <u>warning</u> of what will happen later on.

**2 She takes the sleeping potion**
Juliet gets ready to take the Friar's potion. At first she's afraid it won't work, then worries it'll kill her, or that she'll go mad when she wakes up in the tomb. She imagines she sees Tybalt's ghost looking for Romeo, then drinks the potion. lines 14-58

## I've got a bad feeling about this...

The Friar is helping Juliet out of a <u>sticky situation</u> here — but it's a <u>risky plan</u> too. It's pretty <u>brave</u> of Juliet to take a potion that might kill her. I guess some people will do anything for love.

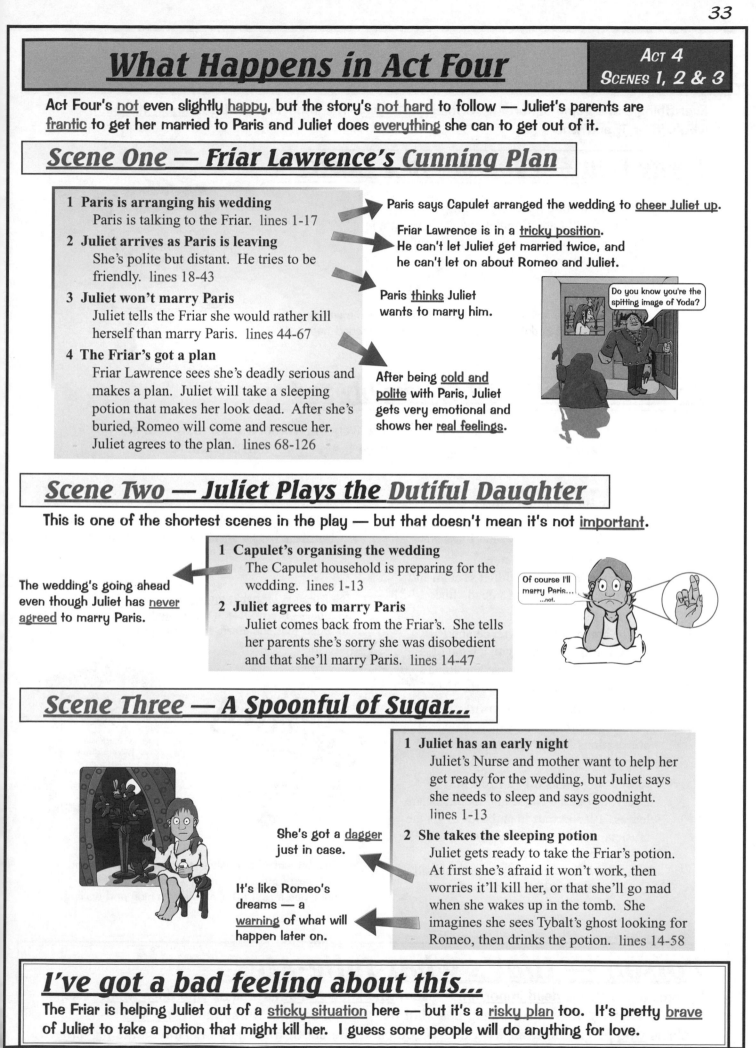

## ACT 4 SCENES 4 & 5 — *What Happens in Act Four*

Everything's still going according to the <u>Friar's plan</u>. It's important that you <u>know the plan</u>, who's <u>in on it</u> and who's <u>not</u>.

## Scene Four — Capulet's in a Fluster

**It's almost time for the wedding**
Capulet, Lady Capulet and the Nurse are in a flurry preparing the house for Juliet and Paris's wedding. lines 1-28

While Juliet's parents are preparing for the wedding, Juliet is doing her best to make sure it won't happen.

## Scene Five — It's All So Terribly Sad

On the surface this scene looks <u>really sad</u>, but the way the Nurse and the Capulets carry on makes it quite <u>funny</u>. A good thing too because the <u>next act</u>'s miserable.

**1 The Nurse thinks Juliet's dead**
The Nurse thinks Juliet is sleeping late, then believes that she's dead. lines 1-16

<u>We</u> know Juliet's going to look dead, but it's the <u>last thing</u> her parents and Nurse expect to see.

**2 Juliet's parents hear the news**
Lady Capulet comes to Juliet's room, and the Nurse tells her Juliet's dead. lines 17-21

The Nurse is probably <u>more upset</u> than anyone — the trouble is she <u>repeats</u> herself so much that she starts to sound <u>daft</u>.

**3 Everyone gets very upset**
Lord Capulet, Friar Lawrence and Paris arrive for the wedding with a band of musicians. Paris, the Nurse and Juliet's parents are all very upset. lines 22-64

**4 The Friar calms them all down**
He takes control of the situation and gets preparations for the funeral under way. lines 65-95

Grave News

Unfortunately Juliet snuffed it last night so the wedding's off. Funeral later today.

**5 The wedding turns into a funeral**
Everyone but the Nurse and the musicians leaves. Peter comes in and tries to get the musicians to play something cheerful. They refuse. Peter insults them, but the musicians win the argument and they all leave. lines 96-138

This bit with the musicians is quite strange, and not very funny. It could be there to give the audience a <u>rest</u> after all the moaning and wailing.

## Poison — that's what Julie-ate...

I promise you this is <u>dead important</u> — learn <u>who knows what</u> as well as <u>who does what</u>. Like the Friar knowing Juliet's not really dead but her parents and the Nurse having <u>no idea</u> — it explains <u>why</u> people do what they do. If you can write about that, you'll hit the marks <u>big-time</u>.

# What Happens in Act Five

The last act! You're a mole's whisker away from knowing the story top to bottom.
But don't start rushing just because it's the last act.

## Scene One — Romeo Gets the Wrong End of the Stick

There's still a tiny chance things will turn out OK for Romeo and Juliet,
but just about everything that could go wrong in Act Five does.

As usual Romeo pays attention to his dreams. He's right to imagine Juliet will kiss him when he's dead, but wrong to think she'll be able to bring him back to life.

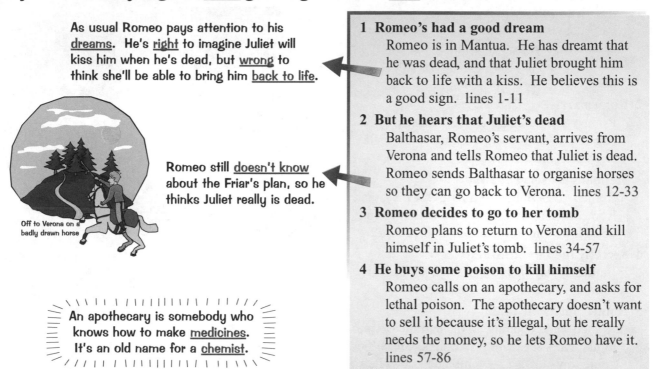

Off to Verona on a badly drawn horse

Romeo still doesn't know about the Friar's plan, so he thinks Juliet really is dead.

An apothecary is somebody who knows how to make medicines. It's an old name for a chemist.

**1 Romeo's had a good dream**
Romeo is in Mantua. He has dreamt that he was dead, and that Juliet brought him back to life with a kiss. He believes this is a good sign. lines 1-11

**2 But he hears that Juliet's dead**
Balthasar, Romeo's servant, arrives from Verona and tells Romeo that Juliet is dead. Romeo sends Balthasar to organise horses so they can go back to Verona. lines 12-33

**3 Romeo decides to go to her tomb**
Romeo plans to return to Verona and kill himself in Juliet's tomb. lines 34-57

**4 He buys some poison to kill himself**
Romeo calls on an apothecary, and asks for lethal poison. The apothecary doesn't want to sell it because it's illegal, but he really needs the money, so he lets Romeo have it. lines 57-86

## Scene Two — The Friar's Letter Didn't Get Through

Here's the first thing to go wrong.

**The Friar's message never got through**
Friar John, Friar Lawrence's messenger to Romeo, comes back from Mantua. He couldn't deliver the letter explaining the Friar's plan. Friar Lawrence decides to be at the Capulet tomb when Juliet wakes up, and to write to Romeo again. lines 1-30

Ahhh, don't shoot the messenger.

Uh-oh — the Friar doesn't think Romeo will have heard about Juliet's death. He doesn't know how urgent it is to find Romeo and tell him what's really going on.

# If only he'd used recorded delivery...

In your essay, show you know the end of the play as well as you know the beginning. Some folks think they can get away with only knowing the beginning in detail. They're wrong. It doesn't matter what essay you're writing, you have to know the whole plot or you'll say something daft.

**ACT 5
SCENE 3**

# What Happens in Act Five

This is it, the <u>last scene</u> of the last act. There are only three scenes in Act 5, but to make up for it Scene 3's a <u>whopper</u>. It's full of misunderstandings and deaths — a proper <u>tragedy</u>.

## Scene Three — Till Death Do Us Part

Another <u>action-packed</u> scene — now with bonus slushy bits.

**1 Paris visits Juliet's grave**
Paris comes to the tomb to say goodbye to Juliet. He says he will come to the tomb every night to lay flowers and mourn. lines 1-17

Romeo has come to <u>prove</u> his love for Juliet. He's come to the tomb to <u>die</u> beside her.

**2 Romeo arrives**
Romeo and Balthasar arrive. Warned by his page, Paris steps away from the tomb so he can watch them. lines 18-21

**3 He sends his servant away**
Romeo gives Balthasar a letter for his father. Romeo tells Balthasar that he will kill him if he follows him into the tomb. lines 22-42

Romeo is <u>tense and desperate</u>.

**4 Secretly the servant stays**
Balthasar stays nearby, worried about Romeo's state of mind. lines 43-44

Paris thinks it's Romeo's <u>fault</u> that Juliet is dead. He thinks she died of <u>grief</u> for Tybalt.

**5 Romeo opens the tomb**
Romeo starts opening up the entrance to the tomb. Paris sees him. He thinks Romeo's going to vandalise the tomb and knows he's meant to be banished from Verona. lines 45-53

The "Watch" is Verona's police force.

Romeo never <u>planned</u> to kill Paris. Paris just <u>gets in the way</u> of his plan to die with Juliet.

Romeo doesn't <u>hate</u> Paris, because they've <u>both</u> had to suffer Juliet's supposed death.

**6 Paris tries to arrest him**
Paris threatens to arrest Romeo. Romeo doesn't recognise him and begs him to go away. lines 54-70

**7 Romeo kills Paris**
They fight. Paris's page runs off to fetch the Watch. Romeo gives Paris a fatal wound. As he dies he asks to be buried alongside Juliet. Romeo agrees. lines 71-74

**8 Romeo puts Paris in the tomb**
Now Romeo recognises Paris and puts him in the tomb. lines 74-87

Romeo's in a <u>terrible hurry</u>. If he waited five minutes, and was alive when Juliet woke up, everything would work out <u>fine</u>.

**9 Romeo kills himself**
Romeo is amazed that Juliet still looks so fresh and alive. He takes his poison and dies. lines 88-120

*O true apothecary!*
*Thy drugs are quick. Thus with a kiss I die.*
*(119-120)*

# What Happens in Act Five

Crumbs, this scene is <u>huge</u>, and pretty complicated too.
Take it one <u>bite-sized chunk</u> at a time and you'll find it <u>easier to swallow</u>.

## Hope You've Got Your Hanky

The Friar's <u>afraid</u> of being caught by the Watch with Romeo and Paris's <u>bodies</u>. If he was less timid here he could <u>stop</u> Juliet from killing herself.

The Watch would <u>stop</u> Juliet from killing herself if they found her.

Lady Montague <u>died</u> in the night, because she was so <u>sad</u> about Romeo's exile.

Nobody seems very surprised that Juliet's <u>died twice</u>.

**10 Friar Lawrence arrives**
The Friar arrives ready to open the tomb. Balthasar comes out of his hiding place and explains that Romeo is already inside. lines 121-143

**11 He sees the bodies**
Friar Lawrence goes into the tomb and sees Paris and Romeo dead. lines 144-146

**12 He tells Juliet to leave**
Juliet wakes up. The Friar realises the plan's gone wrong and wants Juliet to come away from the tomb. She won't leave and he runs. lines 147-159

**13 Juliet kills herself too**
Juliet tries to take poison from Romeo's lips. She hears the Watch coming, and stabs herself with Romeo's dagger. lines 160-170

**14 Everyone's very confused**
The Watch arrive with Paris's Page, and send for the Prince. He quickly arrives, followed by Lord and Lady Capulet. The Watch explain that Paris and Romeo are dead, and Juliet is dead again. lines 171-207

**15 The Prince gets to the bottom of the story**
Montague arrives. The Prince tells him Romeo is dead. The Prince asks for an explanation of what's happened. The Friar tells his part of the story. Balthasar hands over Romeo's letter, which backs up the Friar's story. lines 208-290

**16 The End**
The Prince tells Capulet and Montague that their feud has killed Romeo, Juliet, Mercutio, Tybalt and Paris. Capulet and Montague make peace, and agree to put up gold statues in memory of their children. The Prince asks everyone to leave. lines 291-310

Friar Lawrence says he should be <u>executed</u> if anything is his fault. But he makes everything sound like a big accident so he can't be blamed.

**Phew!**

I'd shake hands if I could change my posture

Go hence, to have more talk of these sad things.
Some shall be pardoned, and some punishèd,
For never was a story of more woe
Than this of Juliet and her Romeo.

(307-310)

## Sniff, sigh — this story makes me tomb miserable...

That's it then, the complete story of '<u>Romeo and Juliet</u>'. The only way to be <u>sure</u> you know it is to see if you can tell the story <u>off by heart</u>. Try it now on your dog. You <u>don't</u> need to memorise it scene by scene, but if you've got a <u>picture</u> of events in <u>each act</u>, your essay will be a winner.

# Revision Summary

Blimey — I never knew 'Romeo and Juliet' was so long and fiddly-complicated. You don't want to get the events of the play in the wrong order when you write your essay — the examiners will think you don't know what you're on about. Try these revision questions, they're delicious. See if you can work through all of them without looking back over the section.

1) Where is the play set?

2) How much does the Prologue to Act 1 tell us about what's going to happen in the play?

3) Who is Romeo in love with in Act 1, Scene 1?

4) Who wants to marry Juliet in Act 1, Scene 2?

5) Why does Benvolio suggest going to the Capulets' party in Act 1, Scene 2?

6) How do Romeo and Benvolio sneak into the party in Act 1, Scene 4?

7) Who wants to fight Romeo at the party?

8) In which scene do Romeo and Juliet meet for the first time?

9) Why is the balcony scene so tense?

10) What does Friar Lawrence hope that the marriage will achieve?

11) Why does the Nurse come to see Romeo in Act 2, Scene 4?

12) Why does Juliet get annoyed with the Nurse when she returns from speaking to Romeo?

13) Give three reasons why Romeo and Juliet can trust Friar Lawrence.

14) Who gets killed in Act 3, Scene 1?

15) What happens to Romeo at the end of Act 3, Scene 1?

16) How does Juliet feel at the end of Act 3, Scene 2? Why?

17) What does Romeo threaten to do in Act 3, Scene 3?

18) What does Friar Lawrence tell Romeo to do in Act 3, Scene 3?

19) What's the turning point in the play that makes it seem impossible that things will work out for Romeo and Juliet?

20) Why does Juliet feel it's so important to get married to Romeo?

21) Explain Friar Lawrence's plan in your own words.

22) In which act and scene does Juliet take the potion?

23) Who finds Juliet and thinks she's dead? Who comes into the bedroom next?

24) Who tells Romeo that Juliet's dead? Who was supposed to deliver the letter?

25) Who's already at the tomb when Romeo arrives? What happens to him?

26) What's the only good thing to come out of the deaths of Romeo and Juliet?

## Three Steps for an Essay

So you've had a good look at the <u>play</u>. In this section we'll look at the kind of <u>essay</u> you'll have to write, and some good tips for getting really <u>good marks</u> in the test.

## Three Steps to Exam Success

These three steps are <u>perfect</u> for answering exam questions. And they work for <u>any kind</u> of Shakespeare question — bargain.

1) Read the question and <u>underline</u> the important bits.

2) Go through the set scenes and look for <u>examples</u> you could use in your answer.

3) Do a quick <u>plan</u> for your essay. Look back at this when you're writing so you don't run out of ideas.

See pages 41-42 for more about planning.

## The Question Will Look Like This

Whichever question type you get, the <u>basic layout</u> will look like this:

### Romeo and Juliet

Act 1 Scene 5, lines 92-126
Act 3 Scene 3, lines 4-108

There might be a bit like this to introduce the <u>topic</u> of the question.

In these scenes, Romeo faces some difficult situations.

**What do Romeo's reactions to these problems reveal about his character?**

*Support your ideas by referring to both of the extracts which are printed on the following pages.*

*18 marks*

This bit tells you which <u>parts of the play</u> the question is about. It'll be about half your set scenes (printed on pages 57-64 of this book).

This basically means "keep looking at the scenes and include loads of <u>quotes</u>".

This is the really important bit — the actual <u>question</u>. It's <u>important</u> that you read this carefully, so that you fully understand what you're being asked.

## Steps? I thought they'd split up...

Although there are a few different types of question (see Section 6), they all pretty much follow the <u>same format</u> as the one on this page. So get familiar with it and you'll know what to expect.

# Using Quotes

For every point you make, you have to back it up by using a <u>quote</u>. Quotes prove your points — if you don't use them, you've got no <u>proof</u> that you're not just making it up.

## Keep the Quotes Short

Keep quotes <u>short</u> and <u>to the point</u> — a couple of lines is usually enough.

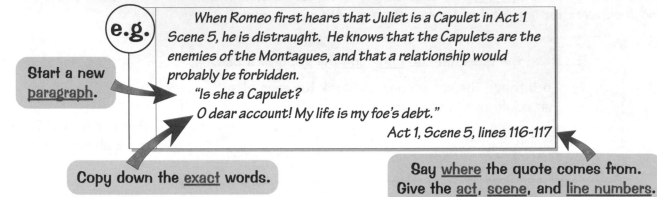

**e.g.** *When Romeo first hears that Juliet is a Capulet in Act 1 Scene 5, he is distraught. He knows that the Capulets are the enemies of the Montagues, and that a relationship would probably be forbidden.*

*"Is she a Capulet?*
*O dear account! My life is my foe's debt."*

Act 1, Scene 5, lines 116-117

Start a new <u>paragraph</u>.

Copy down the <u>exact</u> words.

Say <u>where</u> the quote comes from. Give the <u>act</u>, <u>scene</u>, and <u>line numbers</u>.

If the quote's less than a line you <u>don't</u> need to put it in a separate paragraph or say where the quote's from, but you <u>do</u> need to put it in speech marks.

**e.g.** *Benvolio tries to convince Romeo to leave when they discover Juliet is a Capulet. He says "Away, be gone, the sport is at the best."*

## Explain Why the Quote is Relevant

1) Remember to make it really clear <u>why</u> you've included the quotes — don't just stick them in and expect the examiner to see the point you're making. Always remember in exams to make a point, give an example for it, and explain it.

**e.g.** *When Romeo finds out that he is to be banished, his immediate reaction is that life without Juliet is worse than death: "Ha, banishment! Be merciful, say 'death'". This shows that Romeo is headstrong, and very much in love with Juliet. He would rather die than be without her.*

This quote is good because it shows something about <u>Romeo's character</u>, which is what the question's about.

Sob

2) Quote <u>different characters</u> — this makes your answer more <u>interesting</u>. E.g. You could include Friar Lawrence's view that Romeo has got off lightly with being exiled.

3) Remember though that characters will have particular <u>reasons</u> for saying certain things — don't assume they're being totally honest and fair.

## Status Quote — the studious rock band...

So the main points about quoting are: 1) Keep 'em <u>short</u>. 2) <u>Explain</u> how they answer the question. This'll make sure the quotes really <u>add</u> something to your answer.

# Planning and Structure

If you plan your essay first, you'll have more chance of getting loads of marks.

## You Need a Beginning, a Middle and an End

A good essay has a beginning, a middle and an end. Just like a good story.

Just like me then.

1) The hardest part is beginning your essay. The first sentence has to start answering the question, and tell the examiner that your essay is going to be good. All that from one sentence — so you'd better start practising.

2) The middle part of your essay develops your argument — this is where you make all your points. Follow your plan.

3) The end sums up the points you've made and rounds the essay off nicely.

## Before You Write, Make a Plan

Planning means organising your material to help you write a clear answer that makes sense. A good plan turns that heap of ideas in your head into an argument supported by points.

Planning might seem a pain to do, but if you do it, you'll be less likely to get lost halfway through the essay.

I wish I was organised...

## Five Steps to Planning a Good Essay

1) Work out exactly what the question is asking you to do. Find the key words and underline them.

2) Read the set scenes — highlight quotations you could use.

3) Jot down your ideas — from the set scenes they give you, and from your knowledge of the rest of the play — and then put them into an order.

4) Decide what your opinion is, and how you can use your points to support it — to form an argument. Put your best point first.

5) Don't stick to your plan rigidly. If you think of any more good ideas once you've started writing, then try to fit them in.

## It's the beginning of the end...

If you're not sure what your opinion is, state the arguments for and against, and give evidence to support each viewpoint. Answer the question by comparing the views on each side.

# Planning and Structure

Here's an <u>example</u> of how you could make a plan for a question on <u>Romeo and Juliet</u>.

## Work Out What the Question is Asking

> **(e.g.)** **Act 1 Scene 5, lines 92-126, Act 3 Scene 3, lines 4-108**
>
> In these scenes, Romeo faces some difficult situations.
> **What do Romeo's reactions to these problems reveal about his character?**
> *Support your ideas by referring to both of the extracts which are*
> *printed on the following pages.*

1) Start by <u>underlining</u> the most <u>important</u> words in the question.
   For this one you'd underline "reactions", "character" and "Romeo".

2) Once you've got the question in your head, go through the scenes and <u>pick out sections</u> of the scenes that look like they'll help your answer.

> Hadst thou no poison mixed, no sharp-ground knife,
> No sudden mean of death, though ne'er so mean,
> But 'banishèd' to kill me? 'Banishèd'?
> Act 3, Scene 3, 44-46

3) Go through the scenes again and check for things you <u>might have missed</u> —
   it looks really good if you can find points that are <u>relevant</u> but <u>not obvious</u>.

## Making Your Plan

Next jot down a <u>plan</u> for your essay. <u>Don't</u> bother writing in proper English in your plan — just get your ideas down.

This essay is all about <u>Romeo</u>, so make notes on <u>anything</u> from the scenes you think tells us something about Romeo.

Decide on the best <u>order</u> for your points.

Find some <u>good quotes</u> to back up your points.

Write down any <u>comments</u> you've got on what happens.

*Romeo's character*

1. *<u>He's very determined</u> He continues to love Juliet, even though their families are enemies.*

3. 2. *<u>He's popular and well thought of</u> He is asked to stay at the Capulet banquet despite being a Montague.*
   *"Nay, gentlemen, prepare not to be gone".*
   *He is sentenced to exile instead of death by the Prince as punishment for killing Tybalt.*

2. 3. *<u>He's reckless</u> Romeo says he would rather die than go into exile in Act 3 Scene 3 — exile is worse than death to him. "There is no world without Verona walls".*

## My essay blossomed — I plant it well...

<u>Don't</u> just launch straight in — take the <u>time</u> to plan. Once you've <u>jotted</u> some ideas down,
you'll realise you have <u>more</u> to say than you thought — so there's <u>less</u> reason to <u>panic</u>.
And let's face it, a <u>structured</u> essay will get more marks than one that goes <u>all over the place</u>...

# Writing Your Answer

Once you've got a plan, you're <u>ready</u> to start writing.
Make your points as <u>clearly</u> as you can so the examiner knows what you're on about.

## Write a Simple Opening Paragraph

Start by using the exact <u>words of the task</u> in your introduction.
This shows you've <u>understood</u> the question.

Your introduction <u>doesn't</u> have to be <u>long</u> at all.  It's just there to show what your <u>basic</u> <u>answer</u> to the task is.  In the rest of the paragraphs you'll need to go into <u>detail</u>.

**e.g.**

> <u>*What do Romeo's reactions to these problems reveal about his character?*</u>
>
> *In these scenes we get a strong impression of Romeo's <u>character</u> through his <u>reactions</u> to problems.  He seems to be an intelligent, emotional character, but also one with a fiery and passionate side which leads him to think and do some very dangerous things.*
>
> *We are first introduced to Romeo when...*

The opening sentences use words from the <u>question</u>.

Once you've written your opening paragraph, just follow the order of your <u>plan</u> to write the rest of your essay.

## Make Your Answer Interesting

1) Use <u>interesting</u> words — the examiner will get <u>bored</u> if you <u>overuse</u> dull words and phrases like "nice" and "I think".  Try using words like "<u>fascinating</u>" and phrases like "<u>in my opinion</u>".

2) Keep your style <u>formal</u> — this makes your argument more <u>convincing</u> and gets you even more <u>marks</u>.

3) If you think a passage is "poetic", "realistic" etc., remember to explain <u>exactly why</u> — with examples. <u>Don't</u> assume it's <u>obvious</u> to the examiner.

Boring!
It was a nice day, and everyone had a nice time.

Keep bearing in mind the <u>words</u> used in the <u>question</u>.  Using them in your essay will show you're <u>keeping to the task</u> and not getting lost.

## Allow me to introduce my lovely essay...

Your intro really doesn't need to be anything mindblowing.  Just a couple of sentences to show you've <u>understood</u> the question and to get your answer started.  Then you start moving onto more <u>detailed</u> points in the rest of your answer, with some nice tasty <u>quotes</u> to back them up.

# Concluding and Checking for Errors

Once you've made <u>all</u> your points, you need to <u>sum up</u> your answer and <u>check</u> it through.

## Write a Conclusion to Sum Up Your Key Points

*The conclusion to my speech will be very concise — barely half an hour...*

1) Start a new <u>paragraph</u> for your conclusion.

2) Sum up the <u>main points</u> of your essay <u>briefly</u>. This makes it clear how you've <u>answered</u> the question.

3) Don't go on and on, though. It's best if your conclusion is just a <u>couple of sentences</u>.

## Go Over Your Essay When You've Finished

1) Try to <u>leave time</u> at the end to <u>read through</u> your essay quickly. Check that it <u>makes sense</u>, that you haven't got any facts wrong, and that it says what you <u>want</u> it to say.

*How many more times do I have to go over it?*

2) Check the <u>grammar</u>, <u>spelling</u> and <u>punctuation</u>. If you find a <u>mistake</u>, put <u>brackets</u> round it, cross it out <u>neatly</u> with two lines through it and write the <u>correction</u> above.

> much
> Romeo is very (~~mukh~~) in love with Juliet.

**Don't <u>scribble</u> or put <u>whitener</u> on mistakes — it looks <u>messy</u> and you'll <u>lose marks</u>.**

3) If you've written something which isn't <u>clear</u>, put an <u>asterisk</u> * at the end of the sentence. Put another asterisk in the <u>margin</u>, and write what you <u>mean</u> in the margin.

> *He has been exiled. | Romeo is upset about his punishment*.

## Don't Panic if You Realise You've Gone Wrong

If you realise you've <u>forgotten</u> something really <u>obvious</u> and <u>easy</u>, then write a <u>note</u> about it at the bottom of the <u>final</u> page, to tell the examiner. If there's time, write an extra <u>paragraph</u>. You'll pick up marks for <u>noticing</u> your mistake.

> <u>Don't give up</u> if you're running out of <u>time</u> — even if you only have <u>five minutes</u> left, there's still time to pick up <u>extra marks</u>.

## Check, check, check — I must be rich...

You've almost <u>finished</u>. Keep your conclusions <u>to the point</u>, and <u>check</u> your essay so you don't <u>throw away</u> marks on <u>silly mistakes</u>. Keep a <u>clear head</u> right up to the end — then it's <u>teatime</u>.

# Revision Summary

I like to think of it as the 5 Ps — Planning Prevents Pitifully Poor Performance.  Actually, I think it's a bit more positive than that — Planning Provides Practically Perfect Performance.  The main point is Planning Planning Planning Planning Planning.  Anyway, that's enough Ps for now. On with the revision summary — you only know the answers when you don't have to flick back.

1) Name three useful things you should do before you start writing an answer to an exam question.

2) Why is it important to use lots of quotes in your essay?

3) What three bits of information do you have to give after any quote that's more than a line long?

4) What punctuation must you remember to use for quotes that are shorter than one line?

5) What should you explain about every quote you use?

6) What are the three vital ingredients of a good essay?
   a) Spelling, handwriting and punctuation.
   b) Great ideas, brilliant ideas and fantastic ideas.
   c) A beginning, a middle and an end.

7) What's the big advantage of making a plan for an essay question?

8) If you have a great idea when you're writing your essay which wasn't on your original plan, is it OK to fit it into your essay anyway?

9) How important is it to write your plan in proper English?

10) What do you have to do with the first sentence of the answer?
   a) Give a general answer to the question.
   b) Make your best point straightaway.
   c) Put in a really interesting quote.

11) Should you use mostly formal language or mostly slang in your answer?

12) How long should your closing paragraph be?
   a) About half a page.
   b) As long as a piece of string.
   c) As short as possible but it should include all the main points from the essay.

13) Write down four things you should check for when you read through your essay at the end.

14) How do you correct a spelling mistake?

15) What should you do if you've written something which isn't clear?

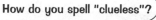
How do you spell "clueless"?

**CHARACTER QUESTIONS**

# Questions About a Character

You might be asked a question about a particular <u>character</u> in 'Romeo and Juliet'.

## Character Questions are Fairly Simple

Questions about a character will often ask you <u>what the scenes show</u> about that person.

**e.g.** Act 1 Scene 5, lines 59-125 and Act 3 Scene 5, lines 87-203
In these scenes we see Lord and Lady Capulet in different situations.
**How do these scenes show different sides of the Capulets' characters?**
*Support your ideas by referring to the scenes.*

When you first read through the question, remember to <u>underline</u> the words which seem the <u>most important</u>.

<u>How</u> do these scenes show <u>different sides</u> of <u>the Capulets' characters</u>?

You have to explain how Shakespeare shows there are different sides to the Capulets.

These words are the most important ones. They tell you what to write about.

## They're Not All Goodies and Baddies

1) The characters in 'Romeo and Juliet' are often more <u>complicated</u> than they seem.

2) Take <u>Lord and Lady Capulet</u>. On the one hand they love Juliet and at the start of the play are happy to let her choose her own husband rather than just <u>choosing</u> one for her. This means they probably <u>trust</u> her. They also want to protect her though — they won't let Paris marry her until she is 15 (in the play Juliet is only 13). They are even happy to let Romeo stay at their banquet in Act 1 Scene 5, even though he is a <u>Montague</u>.

3) BUT — They force her to marry <u>Paris</u> when Tybalt is killed, and Lady Capulet says she wants Romeo <u>dead</u> for killing him.

*Sigh* I'm so bored... I know, I'll go fall in love with the son of my family's arch enemy. That'll be fun!

4) They are also <u>perfectly happy</u> to fight the Montagues, and neither family even try to patch things up with each other until Romeo and Juliet die. They are all pretty <u>stubborn</u>.

5) And then there's <u>Juliet</u>. Although she's generally lovely all the way through the play, she keeps Romeo a <u>secret</u> — refusing to marry Paris and having a strop without really giving her mum and dad a <u>reason</u>. O.K. so it isn't fair for them to arrange Juliet's wedding for her, but you can't really <u>blame</u> them for being a little upset with her <u>reaction</u>.

## Those Capulets, eh? What a couple of characters...

These questions shouldn't ask you anything <u>unexpected</u> — you should know about the characters and their odd little ways before the exam. Try to be really <u>thorough</u> and there'll be no hiccups.

# Characters — The Bigger Picture

If you're asked to write about a <u>character</u> there are <u>a few things</u> you can do to get <u>more marks</u> — it's a question of looking for the <u>less obvious</u> things.

## Think About What Motivates the Characters

1) <u>Motivation</u> means the <u>reasons</u> a character has for acting as they do.

2) The characters in 'Romeo and Juliet' are all after <u>different things</u>. Some people are driven by <u>love</u>, some by <u>hatred</u>. Some of them do things for <u>themselves</u>, some do things for <u>others</u>.

3) For example, Lord and Lady Capulet are motivated by family <u>honour</u> — which is a big theme in the play. They are a <u>noble</u> family and want Juliet to marry honourably into another important noble family. Paris is the <u>perfect</u> choice — he is rich, a <u>count</u> and related to the <u>Prince</u>.

4) Try to show in your answer that you understand what <u>motivates</u> the character you're writing about. Again, find a good <u>quote</u> and say what it tells you about the character:

**e.g.**

> Lady Capulet is sure that arranging a marriage for Juliet will make her happy and help her forget Tybalt's death. She describes Paris as a "gallant, young and noble gentleman", which suggests that she thinks that Paris would make an excellent husband for Juliet.

Have a good look at pages 9-16 for details on the characters and pages 24-37 for a summary of the whole play.

## Remember What Happened in the Past

1) We know <u>more</u> about the characters than just the stuff that happens <u>during</u> the play. Things that happened in the <u>past</u> affect how the characters act towards each other in the play.

2) We know that Romeo is <u>hopelessly romantic</u> before he meets Juliet, because he's <u>pining</u> for Rosaline (his current crush) in Act 1 Scene 1.

3) There's a <u>history</u> of hatred and violence between the <u>Capulets</u> and the <u>Montagues</u>. No one can really <u>remember</u> what the feud between the families is about, but it has a <u>huge effect</u> on the events of the play.

4) Tybalt is so <u>angry</u> at Romeo appearing at the Capulet party in Act 1 Scene 5 that he sets out to <u>kill</u> Romeo in Act 3 Scene 1.

> It fits when such a villain is a guest: I'll not endure him.
>
> Act 1, Scene 5, 74

## Bill Shakes-beer — the nervous pub landlord...

So that's one type of exam question. Writing about characters is probably the <u>simplest</u> of the four kinds of question we'll look at. On the next two <u>pages</u> we'll look at writing about language.

# How Language Is Used

If you're asked about Shakespeare's "use of language", it just means <u>what words he uses</u>.

## Language Can Tell Us About Characters

The kind of words each character uses affects our <u>impression</u> of them.

1) Mercutio is one of the <u>wittiest</u> characters in the play. He's really good with words and quite fun and <u>playful</u>. We can see this in Act 2 Scene 4.

2) The <u>prose</u> (see p.7) Mercutio uses in this scene shows that he's <u>informal</u> and chatty, rather than using <u>verse</u> which would make him seem posh and formal.

> Sure wit! Follow me this jest now till thou hast worn out thy pump, that when the single sole of it is worn, the jest may remain after wearing solely singular.
> Act 2, Scene 4, lines 55-57

Ooh thou art an... um... Ooh...

3) Romeo's language tells us a lot about him as well. When he's talking to Juliet, he talks in verse, using <u>romantic</u> and <u>flowery</u> language (it's all a bit slushy really). Look at the balcony scene in Act 2 Scene 2. You just <u>know</u> Romeo's a <u>hopeless</u> romantic.

> I am no pilot, yet wert thou as far
> As that vast shore washed with the farthest sea,
> I should adventure for such merchandise.
> Act 2, Scene 2, lines 82-84

4) The Nurse is a funny old character and a bit of a <u>windbag</u>. She uses <u>long</u> sentences and <u>repeats</u> things over and over again, which makes her seem <u>old</u> and a bit <u>ridiculous</u>. Bless 'er.

## Language Can be Used to Create Tragedy

Most of the tragic bits in 'Romeo and Juliet' involve people getting killed or being <u>forced</u> to do things <u>against their will</u>. The language they use creates an emotional and <u>tearjerking</u> atmosphere.

**e.g.**
> Death, that hath ta'en her hence to make me wail,
> Ties up my tongue, and will not let me speak.
> Act 4, Scene 5, 31-32

Lord Capulet has just seen Juliet, who appears to be <u>dead</u> after taking the sleeping potion. You can really feel his <u>pain</u> here — he's talking about <u>wailing</u> and not being able to speak through grief. <u>Powerful</u> stuff.

## As long as it's not in Swedish, you'll be fine...

Studying Shakespeare is really <u>all about</u> looking at what language he uses. So if you get a question that asks you specifically about his <u>choice of words</u>, there should be <u>plenty</u> you can write about.

# How Language Creates Mood

"Mood" or "atmosphere" means the <u>feel</u> of a scene — whether it's tense, funny, exciting or whatever. You might be asked about <u>how language is used</u> to create a particular <u>mood</u>.

## Say What Effect the Words Create

**e.g.** **Act 1 Scene 1, lines 1-95 and Act 3 Scene 1, lines 32-87**
How does Shakespeare's choice of language create an angry mood in these fighting scenes?

Use words from the question.

Make it tense... How about some snakes? No...

Say how the language creates a certain effect.

Explain the exact effect of the language.

Quote loads.

> In the first scene, <u>Shakespeare's choice of language creates tension</u> by giving the impression of people shouting and insulting one another in an aggressive way. For example, phrases like "<u>Have at thee, coward!</u>" <u>show us the drama and adrenaline of the fight</u> felt by the people who are caught up in it. Shakespeare uses short sentences with <u>angry</u> language <u>to give the impression of shouting and chaos</u>. When Benvolio shouts "<u>Part, fools!</u>", <u>it adds to the tension by suggesting that he is struggling to be heard above the din of the fighting.</u>
>
> In Act 3 Scene 1, there is less chaos but more tension, and the anger is more personal. Tybalt refers to Romeo as a "<u>villain</u>" and Tybalt is called a "<u>rat-catcher</u>" by Mercutio. The longer sentences and more personal insults used in this scene <u>add to the tension and the sense of hatred between the characters</u>.

Keep the answer focused and to-the-point.

## Look for Mood Changes Within Scenes

It'll add a little <u>extra</u> to your answer if you can identify the place where the mood of a scene <u>changes</u>. For example, if you were writing about Act 3, Scene 1, you could say something like:

> The mood created by the language used by Mercutio and Tybalt in Act 3 Scene 1 is <u>extremely tense</u>. The two characters hurl insults at each other, Mercutio yelling "<u>Zounds, consort!</u>" at Tybalt. This shows that they are on the verge of fighting with each other before Romeo arrives.
>
> <u>When Romeo does arrive, he dramatically changes the feel of the scene</u>. He refuses to fight with Tybalt, instead referring to him as a friend whom he loves "<u>better than thou canst devise</u>". This creates a <u>strange atmosphere</u> in which Tybalt is obviously <u>angry</u> but confused, Mercutio is looking for a fight and Romeo is being very calm and polite, using romantic language instead of the angry language of the other two.

Show how the language reflects the change.

Remember to quote.

Say where the change in mood happens.

## Heaven knows I'm miserable now... but not now...

So there's quite a bit you can write about for these questions to please the examiner. They give you the opportunity to really go to town and show off your <u>understanding</u> of the language.

| THEME QUESTIONS | # Writing About a Theme |

Theme questions sound more tricky than they really are. They're generally just asking <u>how</u> the play puts across a particular <u>message</u> or <u>idea</u>.

## Work Out What the Question is Asking

<u>Theme questions</u> are often worded like this:

> **Act 3 Scene 2, lines 85-end of Scene, and Act 3 Scene 5, lines 65-167**
>
> In the first scene, Juliet learns that Romeo has killed Tybalt and been banished. In the second scene, Juliet refuses to obey her father and marry Paris.
>
> **How do these extracts explore the idea of family loyalty?**
>
> *Support your ideas by referring to the scenes.*

<u>Don't panic</u> if the question seems complicated.

**Read it carefully, and you'll realise it's actually pretty <u>simple</u>.**

> You could rephrase this as:
> "These bits of the play show different attitudes to family loyalty. How do they do this?"

## Theme Questions Aren't as Hard as They Look

1) Read through the scenes with the question in mind, and some points should pretty much <u>leap out</u> at you and give you the <u>basis for a good answer</u>.
   For example, for the question above, this quote from <u>Juliet</u> would be useful:

> NURSE     Will you speak well of him that killed your cousin?
> JULIET     Shall I speak ill of him that is my husband?
> Ah, poor my lord, what tongue shall smooth thy name,
> When I, thy three-hours wife, have mangled it?
> But wherefore, villain, didst thou kill my cousin?
> That villain cousin would have killed my husband.
>                   Act 3, Scene 2, 96-101

2) Once you've found a good extract like this, just say <u>how it relates to the question</u>. Don't forget to stick in some good <u>quotes</u> to back up your points:

Do you wanna knuckle sarnie baldy?

Come on then shorty.

We'll 'ave the lot of yas.

> *Juliet is in a difficult situation in this scene. Her family loyalty means that she has to mourn Tybalt, but she is glad that Tybalt died instead of Romeo. She reminds herself that "That villain cousin would have killed my husband". This shows she feels more loyalty towards Romeo than her own family.*

## I don't like extracts — they remind me of dentists...

Questions about themes generally <u>tell you</u> an opinion, then ask you to <u>prove</u> that it's true. Which makes it <u>easy</u> really — no faffing about deciding what to argue, just find some good <u>evidence</u>.

## Themes You Might be Asked About

Here are a few more things you can do if you get a question about a <u>theme</u> or <u>issue</u> in 'Romeo and Juliet'.

## There are Several Themes in 'Romeo and Juliet'

If you do get a <u>theme question</u>, it's likely to be about one of the following:

> - hatred / the feud
> - love
> - fate
> - family and marriage
> - religion
> - honour

It's worth having a think about these themes and working out <u>what you'd write</u> about them. Have a look at pages 18-23 for more about the <u>themes</u> in 'Romeo and Juliet'.

## Look for the Less Obvious Bits

1) There will usually be plenty of fairly <u>obvious points</u> you can use in your answer to a theme question (like the stuff on the previous page).

2) But if you want to get really <u>great marks</u>, you'll need to go into a bit more <u>detail</u>. Try to write something that answers the question in a way that's <u>not</u> immediately obvious.

> **e.g.**
> *In my opinion this scene shows an uncaring and heartless side to Juliet. Although she mourns Tybalt in Act 3 Scene 2, she also says*
> *"That 'banishèd', that one word 'banishèd',*
> *Hath slain ten thousand Tybalts."*
> Act 3 Scene 2, lines 113-114
> *It seems that Juliet has become so obsessed with Romeo that her family has become unimportant to her — she would rather ten thousand Tybalts died than Romeo was banished.*

3) It's especially important that you give <u>evidence</u> for these kinds of points. The examiner might not have thought of this, so it's <u>vital</u> you back it up with good <u>quotations</u>.

△ Exhibit A

4) Don't go <u>over the top</u> trying to write blindingly original stuff — make sure you don't miss out the <u>clear-cut</u> points that'll give you easy marks. But if you can stick in just <u>one or two</u> more unexpected, well-explained points into your plan, along with the easier stuff, they'll make your answer really <u>stand out</u>.

> Make sure you stick to the question — it's easy to go off the point when you're trying to come up with a really original answer.

## Where do topics go to have fun? A theme park...

You'll <u>never</u> get a question that asks you something unexpected, like "Explore how 'Romeo and Juliet' suggests sword fights are boring". It'll always be a fairly <u>obvious</u> theme, so don't worry.

# Directing a Scene

The <u>fourth</u> type of exam question you might get asks you to imagine you're a <u>director</u> — the person who's <u>in charge</u> of the performance of the play.  These can be fun. Honest.

## As a Director You Can be Creative

If you get a question on how you'd direct a scene, it's a good opportunity to <u>use your imagination</u>. It's all about how to make the play look and sound great <u>on stage</u>.  Here's an example question:

> Act 2 Scene 2 and Act 3 Scene 5
>
> *Imagine you are directing a production of 'Romeo and Juliet'.*
>
> **How would you direct the actors playing Romeo and Juliet in these scenes?**
>
> *Explain your ideas with references to the scenes.*

## Use the Language and Stage Directions

These questions can be a bit <u>scary</u> if you're struggling to think of good ideas. But there will be plenty of <u>clues</u> in the text which will give you some <u>ideas</u>.

1) <u>Look for LINES that stand out</u>

Find some lines that sound <u>dramatic</u> — happy, angry, scary, anything emotional.

Then think about <u>how</u> the actor should say these lines to really give them <u>impact</u>.

2) <u>Look for STAGE DIRECTIONS</u>

These hint at what's happening on stage — e.g. who's <u>moving</u> where, or what <u>effects</u> (e.g. sounds and lighting) there are.

You can <u>interpret</u> these — say <u>how</u> you'd make them happen.

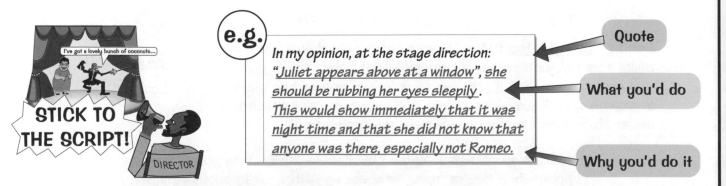

**e.g.**

*In my opinion, at the stage direction:* <u>"Juliet appears above at a window"</u>, *she should be rubbing her eyes sleepily*. *This would show immediately that it was night time and that she did not know that anyone was there, especially not Romeo.*

Quote

What you'd do

Why you'd do it

STICK TO THE SCRIPT!

DIRECTOR

I've got a lovely bunch of coconuts...

## Die-rector — threatening a clergyman?

As with the other questions, you <u>don't</u> have to come up with loads of really <u>groundbreaking</u> ideas — just give some <u>well-explained suggestions</u> with a few more detailed points and you're well away.

# How the Characters Should Speak

It's fair to say that the <u>most important</u> thing about Shakespeare is the <u>words</u> he uses. So as a director, you have to help the actors get the <u>meaning</u> of these words across to the <u>audience</u>.

## Actors Can Say Their Lines in Different Ways

1) Have a think about the <u>meaning</u> of the lines, then decide how you can <u>get this across</u> to the <u>audience</u>. It's all to do with <u>tone of voice</u> — e.g. angry, friendly, sarcastic.

2) There's no right or wrong answer. As long as you <u>explain why</u> you think an actor should speak in a certain way, and give some <u>evidence</u> from the play, you <u>can't go wrong</u>.

3) You can even suggest <u>more than one way</u> for the actor to speak a line — the examiner will like this, as it shows you're <u>thinking</u> really hard about the play. Just make sure you give <u>reasons</u> for each suggestion you make.

 **e.g.**

When Romeo says the lines,

"And what love can do, that dares love attempt: Therefore thy kinsmen are no stop to me."
Act 2 Scene 2, lines 68-69

to Juliet in Act 2 Scene 2, he should be <u>whispering excitedly but quietly</u>. This would show that he is <u>expressing his deepest feelings,</u> and wishes to shout them out, but cannot because he would be heard and caught by the Capulets' guards.

<u>Alternatively</u>, Romeo could be shouting to show that he is madly in love and doesn't care about the danger he is in.

Give an idea about <u>how</u> the lines should be said.

Always <u>explain</u> why you have a certain idea. This is the <u>most important</u> part of your answer.

Give <u>another opinion</u> if you have one.

## You Can Create a Sense of Anticipation

1) <u>Anticipation</u> means wanting to know <u>what will happen next</u>. Shakespeare sometimes creates a feeling of anticipation by letting the <u>audience</u> know something the <u>characters don't</u> — this is called <u>dramatic irony</u>.

**e.g.** Well, girl, thou weep'st not so much for his death As that the villain lives which slaughtered him.
Act 3, Scene 5, 78-79

What's going on?

Ant is a patient.

2) Here, <u>Lady Capulet</u> thinks that Juliet is crying because Tybalt was killed instead of Romeo (who's been <u>exiled</u> by the Prince but is still alive). Really she is crying because Romeo, who we know is her <u>husband</u> (but Lady Capulet doesn't), has had to <u>leave Verona</u>.

3) When writing as a <u>director</u>, you can say how you'd <u>add to the suspense</u> of the scene. E.g. For the bit above, you could show Romeo <u>hiding</u> outside the window (maybe with his head poking round the corner?) <u>listening in and crying</u>.

## Shtop! Thish play is not ready yet...

Being a director means giving your own <u>interpretation</u> of the play. Keep thinking about the effect you want to create on the <u>audience</u> — they're what it's all about. And be <u>enthusiastic</u> — it works.

| DIRECTING QUESTIONS | # How the Characters Should Act |
|---|---|

The director can also create <u>mood</u> for the <u>audience</u> by thinking about how to get the actors to say their <u>words</u> with a bit of feeling.

## Think About How Different Characters Will Act

<u>Different characters</u> will act in different ways. You can <u>compare</u> characters to show how <u>mood</u> is put across to the audience.

**e.g.** *Although both characters should be excited to see each other, Juliet should be a bit more cautious since Romeo has surprised her by showing up unexpectedly. When Romeo says, "stony limits cannot hold love out", he should talk loudly and confidently, <u>to show he is enjoying expressing his emotion and really means it</u>.*

> Show that you know they <u>don't all feel the same</u>.

> Here's your <u>explanation</u> again — really important.

Think about how the characters are <u>feeling</u>, then how to <u>show this</u> in their <u>tone of voice</u>. And remember you can <u>compare</u> different characters and their <u>feelings</u> in the same scene.

## Tell the Actors How to Move

They're actors, so make 'em <u>act</u>. Their <u>body language</u> (gestures, posture and movement) has a big effect on how their characters come across, and you can suggest things that aren't in the stage directions. As ever, <u>explain your ideas</u> and stick to the <u>evidence</u> in the play.

**e.g.** *In Act 3 Scene 5, when Juliet says the lines "Wilt thou be gone? It is not yet near day", the actor playing Juliet should <u>in my opinion</u> be sitting down on her bed, <u>curled up to show that she is upset</u>. Romeo should be standing and looking out of the window <u>to show that he is anxious and thoughtful, and that he knows he must soon leave</u>.*

> Use phrases like "<u>in my opinion</u>" — they show it's <u>your idea</u> and you're <u>exploring</u> the play.

> <u>Expand</u> on your idea.

> Describe the <u>effect</u> you're trying to create.

If you're discussing two <u>different ways</u> to direct a scene, try to <u>link</u> your points together.

> <u>Linking words</u> are dead useful. They help you move from one part of your answer to the next.

- however
- although
- on the other hand
- in comparison

## Get your act together...

So there's <u>a lot to think about</u> in these what-if-you-were-the-director style questions. But they're a really good opportunity to give a good "<u>discussion</u>" — and the <u>more ideas</u> you have, the <u>better</u>.

# Appearance & What Characters Do

Directors have loads of <u>other stuff</u> to think about as well as how the actors should say their lines.

## Mention What Sound and Lighting You'd Use

1) <u>Sound</u> can be used to create a <u>mood</u>. In Act 2 Scene 2, Romeo has broken into the Capulet house — so you could add the sounds of <u>people eating and chatting</u> and <u>Tudor music</u> in the background, to add to the sense of <u>the party going on</u> inside the house.

I said "lighting" not "lightning".

DIRECTOR

2) <u>Lighting</u> is also pretty crucial. Again you can add to what's in the stage directions, e.g. when Juliet appears at the window in Act 2, Scene 2, the rest of the stage could be <u>dimmed</u>, with just the area of the balcony lit up with a <u>soft light</u>. Or have the light shining out of Juliet's <u>window</u>... You're the director, you decide.

3) Remember to <u>explain</u> every suggestion you make. I know I sound like a broken record saying this, but you <u>absolutely, positively, definitely</u> have to do this. Honestly. I really, really mean it.

## Say What Clothes They Should Wear

You can show you understand a scene by talking about the <u>costumes</u> you'd choose for it.

 *e.g.*

*When Romeo enters the Stage in Act 2 Scene 2, he should still be in fancy dress as he has just left the party. The costume would be a bit torn and muddy though as he has just climbed over a wall to get to the balcony. Juliet would be in a nightgown, as she has gone to bed.*

You <u>don't</u> have to stick to <u>old-fashioned</u> costumes. Lots of productions today use <u>modern clothes</u> and you can too — as long as you can show how they <u>suit the characters</u>.

## Use Loads of Quotes (again)

I've got it wrong again, haven't I?

Just like all the other types of question, you absolutely have to use <u>quotes</u> — but it's actually <u>dead easy</u> to stick a few quotes into these questions. <u>Follow these steps</u> and you're sorted:

- say how you want the actors to speak and act, and what lighting and sounds you'd use

- find a quote that backs your idea up and write it down

- say why you'd do it (you won't get the marks otherwise)

## Background music? Sound idea...

Just make sure you're still <u>answering the question</u> — if the question just says "What advice would you give to the actors?", don't go on about the lighting or makeup. But if it just says "How would you direct these scenes?", you can talk about pretty much <u>any aspect</u> of the production.

# Revision Summary

So there you have it. Four types of exam question and oodles of tips to help you with each one. Fair enough, some are easier than others — but you've got to be well prepared for <u>any</u> of those types of question, 'cos you just don't know what'll come up in the exam. And if the sight of the very word "exam" has you breaking out in a cold sweat, it's time to really get learning. Right, enough from me, let's have a butcher's at how much attention you've been paying in this section...

1) If you're writing about a character, is it a good idea or not to give a one-sided description of them? Give your reasons.

2) What does "motivation" mean?

3) What should you think about when writing about a character?

 a) The past

 b) The future

 c) Parallel dimensions

4) What does Shakespeare's "use of language" mean?

5) What's another word for mood?

6) What should you do if you get a theme question that seems really complicated?

 a) Read the question carefully and work out the main thing it's asking.

 b) Write a good answer on a different subject.

 c) Give up school and become a cattle rancher in Bolivia.

7) You don't have to use quotes in theme questions. True or false?

8) Name four themes in 'Romeo and Juliet' you might be asked about.

9) Explain what is meant by:

 a) anticipation

 b) dramatic irony

10) What does "body language" mean?

11) If you talk about clothes, should they always be old-fashioned costumes?

12) Name three things about a production that the director is in charge of deciding.

13) What do you absolutely, positively have to do every time you make a point in an essay?

 a) Explain the point and give evidence.

 b) Say what lighting you'd use.

 c) Play a fanfare.

You could cut the tension with a knife.

The set scenes are the <u>only</u> scenes you need to know in real <u>detail</u>.
Make sure you know these two scenes <u>inside out</u>.

Montague, his wife and Benvolio don't know why Romeo's so sad — Benvolio talks to him and finds out it's because he loves a girl who's sworn never to love anyone.

## Act 1 Scene 1
## Verona.  A public place.
*All exit, except MONTAGUE, LADY MONTAGUE, and BENVOLIO.*

abroach = open

98 'Who started this argument off again?'

by = here

MONTAGUE   Who set this ancient quarrel new abroach?
Speak, nephew, were you by when it began?

BENVOLIO   Here were the servants of your adversary,          100
And yours, close fighting ere I did approach:
I drew to part them — in the instant came

100-109 'Capulet and Montague servants were fighting before I arrived — I tried to split them up but then Tybalt joined the fight. More and more people joined in, until the Prince arrived and stopped it all.'

The fiery Tybalt, with his sword prepared,
Which, as he breathed defiance to my ears,
He swung about his head and cut the winds,          105
Who nothing hurt withal hissed him in scorn:
While we were interchanging thrusts and blows,
Came more and more and fought on part and part,
Till the Prince came, who parted either part.

110-111 'Did you see him today? I'm glad he wasn't involved in this fight.'

fray = fight

LADY MONTAGUE   O, where is Romeo?  Saw you him today?
Right glad I am he was not at this fray.

BENVOLIO   Madam, an hour before the worshipped sun
Peered forth the golden window of the east,

112-124 'I saw Romeo early this morning. He avoided me — I didn't mind because I was feeling a bit depressed myself and reckoned he felt the same way.'

ware = aware/wary

covert = cover

A troubled mind drive me to walk abroad,
Where, underneath the grove of sycamore          115
That westward rooteth from the city side,
So early walking did I see your son.
Towards him I made, but he was ware of me,
And stole into the covert of the wood:
I, measuring his affections by my own,          120
Which then most sought where most might not be found,
Being one too many by my weary self,
Pursued my humour, not pursuing his,
And gladly shunned who gladly fled from me.

125 'He's been seen there a lot recently.'

augmenting = adding to

Aurora = goddess of dawn in Greek mythology

heavy = sad

MONTAGUE   Many a morning hath he there been seen,          125
With tears augmenting the fresh morning's dew.
Adding to clouds more clouds with his deep sighs;
But all so soon as the all-cheering sun
Should in the farthest east begin to draw
The shady curtains from Aurora's bed,          130
Away from the light steals home my heavy son,
And private in his chamber pens himself,

132-136 'He keeps shutting himself in his room during the day. This mood he's in could prove really worrying — unless some good advice snaps him out of it.'

portentous = bad, ominous

Shuts up his windows, locks far daylight out,
And makes himself an artificial night:
Black and portentous must this humour prove,          135
Unless good counsel may the cause remove.

BENVOLIO   My noble uncle, do you know the cause?

139 'Have you questioned him about it properly?'

141-142 'He's his own advisor in love — he keeps his thoughts to himself.'

144-145 'As hard to detect as a worm in an unopened flowerbud.'

148-149 'If we only knew what was wrong, we'd gladly help.'

150-151 'Leave it to me — I'll find out what's bugging him.'

152-153 'I hope you're rewarded by hearing the truth.'

shrift = confession

154 'Is it so early?'

155 'It's just gone nine o'clock.'

155-156 'Blimey. Time goes slow when you're sad. Was that my dad that just left in a hurry?'

I can't believe there's STILL an hour till 'Countdown.'

163-164 'What a shame that the girl who Romeo thinks looks so sweet is actually such a complete cow.'

muffled = obstructed

167-169 'Where shall we eat? Crikey —what fighting happened here? No, don't tell me — I've heard it all before. Hate and love are all mixed up in this.'

170-175 'Nothing's as it should be, everything's in a muddle!' Romeo goes on to list things that are a bit mad, like heavy feathers and cold fires.

MONTAGUE   I neither know it, nor can learn of him.

BENVOLIO   Have you importuned him by any means?

MONTAGUE   Both by myself and many other friends:        140
But he, his own affections' counsellor,
Is to himself — I will not say how true —
But to himself so secret and so close,
So far from sounding and discovery,
As is the bud bit with an envious worm,        145
Ere he can spread his sweet leaves to the air,
Or dedicate his beauty to the sun.
Could we but learn from whence his sorrows grow.
We would as willingly give cure as know.

*Enter* ROMEO

BENVOLIO   See, where he comes.  So please you, step aside;
I'll know his grievance, or be much denied.

MONTAGUE   I would thou wert so happy by thy stay,
To hear true shrift.  Come, madam, let's away.

*Exit* MONTAGUE *and* LADY MONTAGUE

BENVOLIO   Good morrow, cousin.

ROMEO                                              Is the day so young?

BENVOLIO   But new struck nine.

ROMEO                                Ay me!  Sad hours seem long.  155
Was that my father that went hence so fast?

BENVOLIO   It was.  What sadness lengthens Romeo's hours?

ROMEO   Not having that, which, having, makes them short.

BENVOLIO   In love?

ROMEO   Out —                                              160

BENVOLIO   Of love?

ROMEO   Out of her favour where I am in love.

BENVOLIO   Alas that love so gentle in his view,
Should be so tyrannous and rough in proof!

ROMEO   Alas, that Love, whose view is muffled still,        165
Should, without eyes, see pathways to his will!
Where shall we dine?  O me!  What fray was here?
Yet tell me not, for I have heard it all.
Here's much to do with hate, but more with love.
Why, then, O brawling love, O loving hate,        170
O anything, of nothing first create!
O heavy lightness, serious vanity,
Misshapen chaos of well-seeming forms!
Feather of lead, bright smoke, cold fire, sick health!
Still-waking sleep, that is not what it is!        175
This love feel I, that feel no love in this.
Dost thou not laugh?

Section 7 — The Set Scenes

BENVOLIO                    No, coz, I rather weep.

ROMEO   Good heart, at what?

BENVOLIO                    At thy good heart's oppression.

ROMEO   Why, such is love's transgression.

    Griefs of mine own lie heavy in my breast,                    180

    Which thou wilt propagate, to have it pressed

    With more of thine; this love that thou hast shown

    Doth add more grief to too much of mine own.

    Love is a smoke raised with the fume of sighs,

    Being purged, a fire sparkling in lovers' eyes,                    185

    Being vexed a sea nourished with lovers' tears:

    What is it else?  A madness most discreet,

    A choking gall and a preserving sweet.

    Farewell, my coz.

BENVOLIO               Soft! I will go along;

    And if you leave me so, you do me wrong.                    190

ROMEO   Tut, I have lost myself; I am not here,

    This is not Romeo, he's some other where.

BENVOLIO   Tell me in sadness, who is that you love.

ROMEO   What, shall I groan and tell thee?

BENVOLIO                              Groan! Why no,

    But sadly tell me, who?                    195

ROMEO   Bid a sick man in sadness make his will?

    Ah, word ill urged to one that is so ill.

    In sadness, cousin, I do love a woman.

BENVOLIO   I aimed so near, when I supposed you loved.

ROMEO   A right good mark-man!  And she's fair I love.                    200

BENVOLIO   A right fair mark, fair coz, is soonest hit.

ROMEO   Well, in that hit you miss: she'll not be hit

    With Cupid's arrow, she hath Dian's wit;

    And, in strong proof of chastity well armed,

    From love's weak childish bow she lives uncharmed.                    205

    She will not stay the siege of loving terms,

    Nor bide th'encounter of assailing eyes,

    Nor ope her lap to saint-seducing gold:

    O, she is rich in beauty, only poor,

    That when she dies with beauty dies her store.                    210

BENVOLIO   Then she hath sworn that she will still live chaste?

ROMEO   She hath, and in that sparing makes huge waste,

    For beauty starved with her severity

    Cuts beauty off from all posterity.

    She is too fair, too wise, wisely too fair,                    215

    To merit bliss by making me despair:

    She hath forsworn to love, and in that vow

    Do I live dead that live to tell it now.

coz = cousin

179-183 'Love is a bit depressing. That's life.  Don't feel bad for me — your worry will make me feel guilty and even more depressed.'

propagate = make bigger

purged = cleared away

vexed = annoyed

187-188 'What else is it? A wise madness, a deadly poison, a healing medicine.'

gall = poison

189 'Hang on, I'll come with you.'

191-192 'Hmm. I'm not feeling myself.  I'm not here, this isn't Romeo, he's somewhere else.'

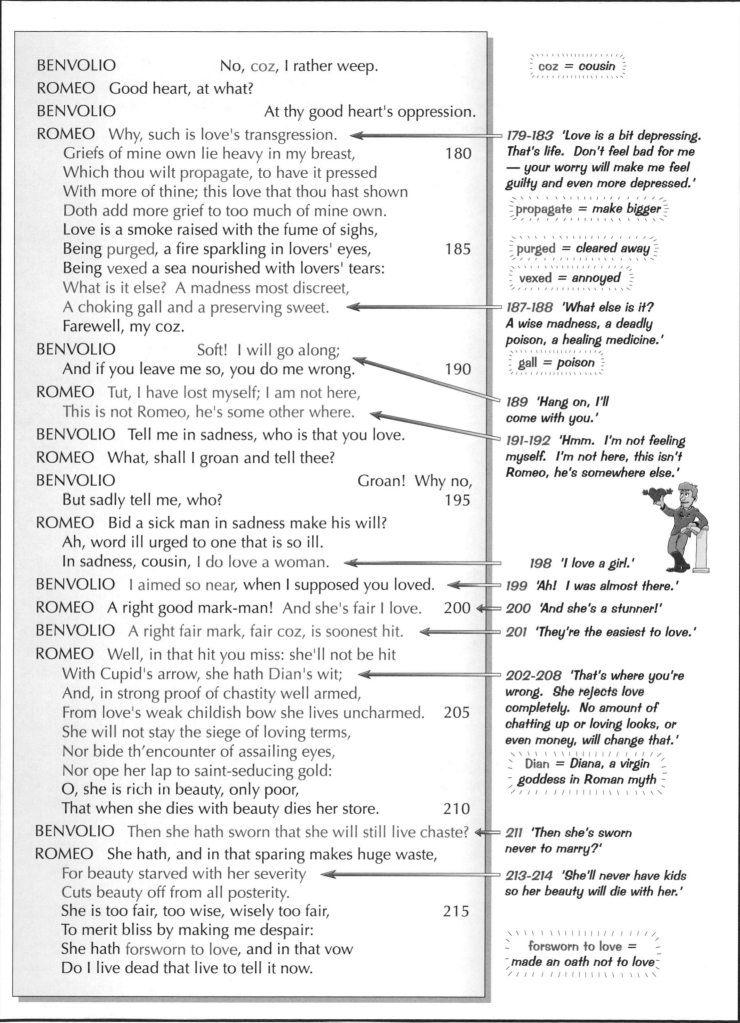

198 'I love a girl.'

199 'Ah! I was almost there.'

200 'And she's a stunner!'

201 'They're the easiest to love.'

202-208 'That's where you're wrong.  She rejects love completely.  No amount of chatting up or loving looks, or even money, will change that.'

Dian = Diana, a virgin goddess in Roman myth

211 'Then she's sworn never to marry?'

213-214 'She'll never have kids so her beauty will die with her.'

forsworn to love = made an oath not to love

220 'How can I forget her?'

221-222 'You should take a look at some other good-looking girls.'

Phwoar!

226-230 'She can't be forgotten that quickly — seeing another pretty girl would only remind me of her.'

pay that doctrine = teach you that lesson

BENVOLIO   Be ruled by me, forget to think of her.

ROMEO   O, teach me how I should forget to think.                    220

BENVOLIO   By giving liberty unto thine eyes;
   Examine other beauties.

ROMEO                             'Tis the way
   To call hers, exquisite, in question more:
   These happy masks that kiss fair ladies' brows,
   Being black puts in mind they hide the fair;                      225
   He that is strucken blind cannot forget
   The precious treasure of his eyesight lost:
   Show me a mistress that is passing fair,
   What doth her beauty serve, but as a note
   Where I may read who passed that passing fair?                    230
   Farewell: thou canst not teach me to forget.

BENVOLIO   I'll pay that doctrine, or else die in debt.

*Exeunt*

## Act 2  Scene 2
## Capulet's orchard

ROMEO *comes forward.*

ROMEO   He jests at scars that never felt a wound.

*1 'Only someone who's never been in love jokes about it.'*

JULIET *appears above at a window*

But soft, what light through yonder window breaks?
It is the east, and Juliet is the sun.
Arise, fair sun, and kill the envious moon,
Who is already sick and pale with grief          5
That thou, her maid, art far more fair than she.
Be not her maid, since she is envious,
Her vestal livery is but sick and green,
And none but fools do wear it; cast it off.
It is my lady, O it is my love!                  10
O that she knew she were!
She speaks, yet she says nothing; what of that?
Her eye discourses, I will answer it.
I am too bold, 'tis not to me she speaks.
Two of the fairest stars in all the heaven,      15
Having some business, do entreat her eyes
To twinkle in their spheres till they return.
What if her eyes were there, they in her head?
The brightness of her cheek would shame those stars,
As daylight doth a lamp.  Her eyes in heaven     20
Would through the airy region stream so bright
That birds would sing and think it were not night.
See how she leans her cheek upon her hand!
O that I were a glove upon that hand,
That I might touch that cheek!

JULIET                              Ay me!

ROMEO (*Aside*)                     She speaks.  25
O speak again, bright angel, for thou art
As glorious to this night, being o'er my head,
As is a wingèd messenger of heaven
Unto the white-upturnèd wondering eyes
Of mortals that fall back to gaze on him,        30
When he bestrides the lazy-passing clouds,
And sails upon the bosom of the air.

JULIET   O Romeo, Romeo, wherefore art thou Romeo?
Deny thy father and refuse thy name.
Or if thou wilt not, be but sworn my love,       35
And I'll no longer be a Capulet.

ROMEO (*Aside*)   Shall I hear more, or shall I speak at this?

*4-6 'Rise, Sun, and send the envious moon away, who's already annoyed that you, her servant, are more beautiful than she is.'*

*8-9 'Her virgin's appearance is sick and green, and only fools wear that look; throw it off.'*

*discourses = talks to me*

*15-17 'Her eyes could take the place of two of the most beautiful stars in heaven.'*

*18-19 'If those stars took the place of her eyes, her cheeks' brightness would shame them.'*

*stream = shine*

*29 'The eyes turned up so you can mainly see the whites.'*

*33-34 'Why are you Romeo? Deny your dad, and refuse to call yourself Montague.'*

38-39 'Only your name is my enemy. You'd still be you, even if you weren't called Montague.'

JULIET  'Tis but thy name that is my enemy —
Thou art thyself, though not a Montague.
What's Montague?  It is nor hand nor foot,  40
Nor arm nor face, nor any other part
Belonging to a man.  O be some other name!
What's in a name?  That which we call a rose

43-44 'A rose would still smell as nice even if it had a different name.'

By any other word would smell as sweet;
So Romeo would, were he not Romeo called,  45
Retain that dear perfection which he owes
Without that title.  Romeo, doff thy name,

doff = take off

48-49 'and instead of your name take me.'

And for thy name, which is no part of thee,
Take all myself.

ROMEO                   I take thee at thy word.
Call me but love, and I'll be new baptised;  50
Henceforth I never will be Romeo.

JULIET  What man art thou that thus bescreened in night

bescreened = hidden

53 'interrupts my private thoughts'

So stumblest on my counsel?

ROMEO                              By a name

53-56 'I don't know how to say who I am using a name.  I hate it because it's your enemy's.'

I know not how to tell thee who I am.
My name, dear saint, is hateful to myself,  55
Because it is an enemy to thee;
Had I it written, I would tear the word.

58-59 'You haven't even said 100 words and I know who you are.'

JULIET  My ears have yet not drunk a hundred words
Of thy tongue's uttering, yet I know the sound.
Art thou not Romeo, and a Montague?  60

ROMEO  Neither, fair maid, if either thee dislike.

62 'How did you get here and why?'

JULIET  How camest thou hither, tell me, and wherefore?
The orchard walls are high and hard to climb,
And the place death, considering who thou art,
If any of my kinsmen find thee here.  65

kinsmen = relatives

66 'I flew over these walls with a lover's wings'

ROMEO  With love's light wings did I o'erperch these walls,
For stony limits cannot hold love out,

68 'Whatever love can do, it'll dare to try.'

And what love can do, that dares love attempt:
Therefore thy kinsmen are no stop to me.

JULIET  If they do see thee, they will murder thee.  70

ROMEO  Alack, there lies more peril in thine eye
Than twenty of their swords. Look thou but sweet,
And I am proof against their enmity.

peril = danger

proof = armoured

enmity = hatred

JULIET  I would not for the world they saw thee here.

76 'Unless you love me, let them find me here.'

ROMEO  I have night's cloak to hide me from their eyes,  75
And but thou love me, let them find me here.

77-78 'If I don't have your love, it'd be better if I were killed than my death put off.'

My life were better ended by their hate,
Than death proroguèd, wanting of thy love.

JULIET  By whose direction found'st thou out this place?

ROMEO   By Love, that first did prompt me to inquire:     80
    He lent me counsel, and I lent him eyes.
    I am no pilot, yet wert thou as far
    As that vast shore washed with the farthest sea,
    I should adventure for such merchandise.

JULIET   Thou knowest the mask of night is on my face,     85
    Else would a maiden blush bepaint my cheek
    For that which thou hast heard me speak tonight.
    Fain would I dwell on form, fain, fain deny
    What I have spoke, but farewell compliment.
    Dost thou love me?  I know thou wilt say 'Ay',     90
    And I will take thy word; yet if thou swear'st,
    Thou mayst prove false: at lovers' perjuries
    They say Jove laughs.  O gentle Romeo,
    If thou dost love, pronounce it faithfully.
    Or if thou think'st I am too quickly won,     95
    I'll frown and be perverse, and say thee nay,
    So thou wilt woo, but else not for the world.
    In truth, fair Montague, I am too fond,
    And therefore thou mayst think my behaviour light:
    But trust me, gentleman, I'll prove more true     100
    Than those that have more coying to be strange.
    I should have been more strange, I must confess,
    But that thou overheard'st, ere I was ware,
    My true-love passion — therefore pardon me,
    And not impute this yielding to light love,     105
    Which the dark night hath so discoverèd.

ROMEO   Lady, by yonder blessèd moon I vow,
    That tips with silver all these fruit-tree tops —

JULIET   O swear not by the moon, th'inconstant moon,
    That monthly changes in her circled orb,     110
    Lest that thy love prove likewise variable.

ROMEO   What shall I swear by?

JULIET                           Do not swear at all.
    Or if thou wilt, swear by thy gracious self,
    Which is the god of my idolatry,
    And I'll believe thee.

ROMEO                      If my heart's dear love —     115

JULIET   Well, do not swear.  Although I joy in thee,
    I have no joy of this contract tonight,
    It is too rash, too unadvised, too sudden,
    Too like the lightning, which doth cease to be
    Ere one can say 'It lightens'.  Sweet, good night.     120
    This bud of love, by summer's ripening breath,
    May prove a beauteous flower when next we meet.

counsel = advice

82-84 'I'm not a sailor, but even if you were as far away as the furthest away sea, I would risk the journey for you.'

bepaint = paint, colour

fain = gladly

88-92 'I'd gladly deny what I just said, but forget the normal rules.  Do you love me?  I know you'll say "yes", and I'll believe you — but if you swear it you might be proved to be a liar.'

92-93 'They say the god Jove laughs at lies told by lovers.'

95-97 'If you think I've given in too easily, I'll frown, get cross and say no, so you have to persuade me, otherwise I won't.'

98 'I'm too in love'

light = careless

coying = skill at flirting

strange = aloof

ware = aware

104-105 'Therefore forgive me and don't think my surrender to you is careless love.'

Oi!  Romeo! You're ace!

lest = in case

gracious = having all the graces of body and spirit

idolatry = worshipping idols instead of God

You're not so bad yourself, chuck!

116-117 'Although you make me happy, I'm not happy about making these promises tonight.'

120-122 She's saying this is a good start but that's enough for now.

64

repose = relaxation

Are you going to tell me you love me?

vow = promise

129 'I wish I had my vow back to give it again.'

frank = generous

bounty = generosity

134-135 'The more love I give you, the more love I get back since both of them are endless amounts.'

adieu = goodbye

anon = coming!

afeard = afraid

140-141 'This is only a dream, too wonderful to be real.'

143-146 'If the intention of your love is honourable, and you want to marry me, send me a message tomorrow through someone I'll send, to say where and when the ceremony will happen.'

beseech = ask

151 & 152 = 'I ask you... to stop loving me and leave me to my sadness.'

thrive = prospers

See ya! I've gotta go!

156-157 'Love goes to love like kids leaving school (happy), but it goes away from love like kids going to school (grumpy).'

Good night, good night! as sweet repose and rest
Come to thy heart as that within my breast.

ROMEO   O wilt thou leave me so unsatisfied?   125

JULIET   What satisfaction canst thou have tonight?

ROMEO   Th'exchange of thy love's faithful vow for mine.

JULIET   I gave thee mine before thou didst request it,
And yet I would it were to give again.

ROMEO Wouldst thou withdraw it?  For what purpose, love?

JULIET   But to be frank and give it thee again,
And yet I wish but for the thing I have.
My bounty is as boundless as the sea,
My love as deep; the more I give to thee
The more I have, for both are infinite.   135

            NURSE calls within

I hear some noise within.  Dear love, adieu! —
Anon, good Nurse!  Sweet Montague, be true.
Stay but a little, I will come again.

            Exit above

ROMEO   O blessèd, blessèd night!  I am afeard,
Being in night, all this is but a dream,   140
Too flattering-sweet to be substantial.

            Enter JULIET above

JULIET   Three words, dear Romeo, and good night indeed.
If that thy bent of love be honourable,
Thy purpose marriage, send me word tomorrow,
By one that I'll procure to come to thee,   145
Where and what time thou wilt perform the rite,
And all my fortunes at thy foot I'll lay,
And follow thee my lord throughout the world.

NURSE (Within)   Madam!

JULIET   I come, anon.  But if thou meanest not well,   150
I do beseech thee —

NURSE (Within)            Madam!

JULIET                    By and by I come —
To cease thy strife, and leave me to my grief.
Tomorrow will I send.

ROMEO   So thrive my soul —

JULIET                    A thousand times good night!
            Exit above

ROMEO   A thousand times the worse, to want thy light.   155
Love goes toward love as schoolboys from their books,
But love from love, toward school with heavy looks.

*Section 7 — The Set Scenes*

# Index

# *Index*